LAO - TZU'S
WHISPERS OF WISDOM

THE **TAO**

SPEAKS

Adapted and Illustrated by Tsai Chih Chung
Translated by Brian Bruya

ANCHOR BOOKS
DOUBLEDAY
New York London Toronto Sydney Auckland

AN ANCHOR BOOK
PUBLISHED BY DOUBLEDAY
A division of Bantam Doubleday Dell Publishing Group, Inc.
1540 Broadway, New York, New York 10036

ANCHOR BOOKS, DOUBLEDAY, and the portrayal of an anchor
are trademarks of Doubleday,
a division of Bantam Doubleday Dell Publishing Group, Inc.

Library of Congress Cataloging-in-Publication Data
Ts'ai, Chih-chung, 1948-
The Tao Speaks: Lao-tzu's Whispers of Wisdom/adapted and illustrated by
Tsai Chih-chung; translated by Brian Bruya.
p. cm.
1. Lao-tzu —Caricatures and cartoons. I. Title
BL1930.T7213 1995
299'.51482 —dc20   94-33828
CIP

ISBN 0-385-47259-5
Copyright © 1995 by Tsai Chih Chung
Translation Copyright © 1995 by Brian Bruya

Contents

Editor's Note

For the sake of familiarity, we have chosen to use the old spellings for *Dao (Tao)* and *Laozi (Lao-tzu)* in the title and the subtitle of this book; apart from these two exceptions, the rest of the book employs the new *pinyin* system of spelling, as do the earlier books in this series. Please see the Translator's Preface that follows for further elucidation of this new system.

Translator's Preface

The mere novelty of an illustrated version of a Chinese classic deserves a brief explanation.

Tsai Chih Chung (C.C. Tsai) is the most accomplished and popular cartoonist in all of East Asia, and several of his books have even been incorporated into the public school curriculum in Japan. C.C. Tsai began his career at the age of sixteen by publishing the first of what would be approximately 200 "action" comic books. Following that, he went into animation and garnered himself the Chinese equivalent of our Oscar while building up the largest animation company in Taiwan. In his spare time, he turned to the humor of comic strips and put out the first daily comic strip in Taiwan newspapers.

Then, one day on a flight to Japan, he began to sketch scenes from a book he was reading. The book had been written over two thousand years ago by one of the most influential thinkers in Chinese history, the famous Daoist (Taoist) thinker named Zhuangzi (Chuang-tzu). From these sketches emerged a new genre in the book world — a serious (though lighthearted) comic book explicating a profound topic. C.C.'s aim was not to simplify, but to clarify. The ancient language in China is difficult for modern people to understand, so in addition to illustrating the subject matter, he also rendered the text into Modern Chinese.

When *Zhuangzi Speaks* came out in Taiwan, it shot to the top of the bestseller list, and the head of a major publishing company immediately remarked that it had world potential. Tired of animation by now, C.C. sold off his company and devoted all of his efforts to the daily comic strips and his new series on ancient Chinese thought, both of which were bringing him unparalleled fame for a cartoonist. Soon he held the four highest spots atop the bestseller list, until other authors demanded that comic books no longer be allowed on the list of "serious literature." There are now over twenty books in C.C.'s series and millions of copies in print, and, just as predicted, they are rapidly gaining popularity all over the world.

The Tao Speaks is a close adaptation of a book known as the *Dao De Jing*, which is attributed to a mysterious figure known as Laozi. *"Dao De Jing"* literally means "The Classic of the Way and the Virtue." In this book, the word *"Dao"* is used more in a metaphysical sense, as an insentient and unseen force or principle, than in the concrete (or metaphorical) sense of a pathway, and since there is no convenient English rendering of this sense of the word, I leave it simply as "the Dao." *"De"* on the other hand is a bit more complicated.

I translate *"De"* as "virtue," but the meanings of the words *"De"* and "virtue " are similiar in more than just one sense. They both have the meaning of moral excellence according to a certain standard, yet there is still more to them than just this. In the *Dao De Jing*, "virtue" is also used in a metaphysical sense, as a kind of power of the Dao that nurtures or is immanent in all things. For this reason some translators have rendered it as "power" or "potency." Interestingly, if we look up "virtue" in the *Oxford English Dictionary*, the very first definition reads: "The power or operative influence in a supernatural or divine being." The dictionary reminds us that this is an archaic definition, but for purposes here, we will go back to it. Keep in mind, then, that "virtue" in the *Dao De Jing* means 1) moral excellence according to the standard of the Dao, and 2) a kind of nurturing potency stemming from the Dao and inherent in all things. In Daoism, the most natural person is the most virtuous person.

Any reader who has come across Daoism before may be wondering why it is written here as "Dao" rather than the more common spelling "Tao." The reason for this is that one system of Romanization (examples of which are *"Tao Te Ching"* and "Lao-tzu") gained almost universal acceptance for a time, but then China switched to a different system, and the rest of the world has been trying to catch up ever since. I use this relatively new system, called *pinyin*, and that is why here you see *"Dao De Jing"* and "Laozi." It is not really an issue of which system is better, but to the uninitiated, the examples above from the new system are certainly less misleading than those of the old system.

There are several places in this book (p. 32, for instance) where C.C. draws what looks like a tiny, gleaming hat. This is actually a depiction of a Chinese ingot — a quantity of precious metal, symbolic here of treasure or wealth.

The panels at the margin of each page appeared in the Chinese version as supplementary material. We retain them not because the information is essential but primarily because they add a nice decorative touch to the book.

Many thanks to Professor Lian Xinda for again vetting the manuscript and offering numerous useful corrections. Thanks also to Professor Michael LaFargue for providing a lucid and enlightening introduction.

- B.B.

Introduction

The origins of the *Dao De Jing* (*Tao Te Ching*), on which *The Tao Speaks* is based, are shrouded in mystery. The earliest manuscript[1] has no title and names no author. Most critical scholars today think it is a collection of sayings from an oral tradition, rather than the work of any single individual, and that its traditional author Laozi (or Lao-tzu, literally "Old Master") may not have been an historical person. Perhaps the best one can do by way of historical introduction, therefore, is first to sketch the general situation in China about the time the *Dao De Jing* was written (circa 350–250 B.C.), and then make some suggestions as to how the *Dao De Jing* came into being.

An outline of contemporary Chinese history:

During the period from roughly 1000–700 B.C., China was unified under the rule of a single Emperor of the Zhou Dynasty. The Zhou Empire was divided into many smaller states, with each state governed by a noble family who ruled on behalf of the Emperor, in a system similar to the "feudal" order of medieval Europe. An idealized picture of this "united China" maintained its hold on Chinese thinkers long after the system itself had disintegrated.

Starting in the eighth century B.C., the Zhou Empire began to disintegrate. The Emperor lost all effective control. Noble families within each state competed with the official ruling family for power, and the heads of the various states waged constant territorial wars against each other, each vying to reunite the now fragmented empire under his own rule. Over time, larger states swallowed up smaller ones, so that by 300 B.C. only seven large states remained. The latter part of this era is called the "Warring States" period because of the great unrest. However, this period was also a time of con-siderable material progress and prosperity. And the self-destruction of the nobility during this time gave rise to great opportunities for those lower on the social scale to advance to positions of power, influence, and wealth. One of these groups was a class of men called *shi*, drawn from ambitious peasantry or dispossessed nobility, who became professional soldiers, administrators, and advisors to the new rulers of the various states during this period.[2] It is from this group that most classical Chinese philosophers came.

The Warring States period came to an end in 221 B.C. when a military leader from the Western state of Qin conquered the other states and reunited the empire under his military dictatorship. His dynasty was subsequently replaced in 206 B.C. by the Han dynasty (206 B.C.–220 A.D.), and it was this dynasty that finally established the pattern of Chinese political organization that was to last until 1912: an Emperor who ruled through a large corps of elite, specially trained bureaucrats, open (in theory at least) to all ranks of Chinese society. It was this corps that inherited the role of Warring States *shi*.

The hundred schools contend.

Some Warring States *shi* undoubtedly focused on purely practical matters. But others were very idealistic, and had hopes to reform Chinese political life by infusing it with high moral and spiritual ideals. They intended to do this through the administrative positions they aspired to hold, and through the advice they hoped to offer to contemporary rulers. The earliest and most famous of such idealistic *shi* was the group that gathered around Confucius (Kongzi, circa 550–480 B.C.). By the time of the Warring States there were probably hundreds of such small groups of men, typically gathered around one or more highly respected *shi* teachers, often traveling from state to state hoping to gain positions of influence where they could convince local rulers to reform their policies. Intense discussion within, and debates between, these groups gave rise to most of what we know today as classical Chinese philosophy.

There were several groups who claimed to practice "the Dao of Confucius," emphasizing Benevolence, Uprightness (Righteousness), and Etiquette (Propriety), and supporting family loyalties and social amenities. The Mohists, a very large and well organized group capable of deploying its own private army to come to the aid of unjustly victimized states, emphasized a utilitarian social morality motivated by love for all people equally. The *fa-jia* (usually translated as "realists" or "legalists") devised political strategies based on analysis of political and economic forces, and emphasized legal and administrative governmental structure rather than the personal virtue of the ruler. Attempts by these groups to formulate doctrines and counter-doctrines gave rise to a specialized focus on language, stimulating the earliest Chinese "logicians."[3] Most of the philosophers known to us from this period were greatly preoccupied with questions of leadership and social organization. Other *shi,* however, became disillusioned and withdrew from political life entirely. Among these are some Daoist groups described in the *Zhuangzi (Chuang-tzu)*, another book roughly contemporary with the *Dao De Jing* and expressing similar ideas.

The opening paragraph of Chapter 15 of the *Zhuangzi* contains the following description of the several main lifestyles adopted by different groups of Warring States *shi:*

[*Shi* who, out of scrupulous concern for their moral integrity, refuse to have anything to do with politics:] To have strict ideals and high-minded ways, to feel alien from the times and different from the ordinary masses, to discourse loftily and criticize vindictively, interested only in their strong convictions—this describes the ways favored by the *shi* of mountains and valleys, men who condemn the age, and who wither away or drown themselves [in despair].

[High-minded Confucian reformers:] To preach Benevolence and Uprightness . . . being respectful, temperate, modest, deferential, interested only in improving themselves—this de-

scribes the ways favored by *shi* who go putting the world to rights, the men who teach and advise, the "Learners" both of the wandering and the stay-at-home kind.

[Egotistic *shi* and political schemers:] To talk of great achievements and establishing great reputations, to make ruler and minister observe the formalities, and reform the ways both of superior and subject, interested only in maintaining order—these are the ways preferred by *shi* at court, men who put kings on their thrones and strengthen their states, those who achieve great successes, conquering more territories.

[*Shi* who have withdrawn from the world to live a simple and happy private life:] To head for the woods and marshes, dwell in the unsettled wilderness, just fish and live untroubled, interested only in Doing Nothing [wu wei]— these are the ways preferred by *shi* of the rivers and seaside, men who shun the times, untroubled idlers.

[*Shi* who became preoccupied with various yogic techniques for strengthening vital energy and increasing longevity:] To huff and puff, exhale and inhale, blow out the old breath and draw in the new, practice the "bear-hang" and the "bird-stretch" postures, interested only in attaining long life—these are the ways preferred by *shi* of "guide-and-pull" exercises, men who nurture their bodies, hoping to live as long as Grandfather Peng.

The *Dao De Jing*.

The *Dao De Jing* shows an acquaintance with most of the schools and attitudes described above, incorporating some of these views into its own vision, while criticizing others. How did the book originate, and what is its message? Modern scholars are divided on this issue. Most scholars in the past regarded this book as the work of a single thinker, a philosopher or mystic. Some scholars see him as someone very frightened by the chaos and danger of the Warring States period, and preoccupied with devising strategies for achieving personal security. Others see him as a radical social critic, attacking the entire feudal political system and advocating a return to a more primitive communal society. Still others see him as the first metaphysician in China, discovering (perhaps through mystical insight) the Dao as the ultimate Ground of Being underlying all visible phenomena. And finally, some think that the paradoxes in the *Dao De Jing* are meant simply to undermine all human value judgments, teaching us a radical skeptical relativism.

These difficulties in interpretation are due partly to the form of the book. It does not consist of organized essays, but a collection of terse aphorisms and comments strung together with very little indication as to how they are connected. Different interpreters see different passages as central to its message, and have different ways of relating various passages to one another. In addition, some see contradictions in the book, compounding problems for interpretation. Those who think the Dao is an Ultimate Family beyond all determinations and dualities (like the Brahman of Hinduism), for example, have difficulty with the fact that the *Dao De Jing* is clearly ("dualistically") partial to Softness, Femininity, and Emptiness, in contrast to Hardness, Masculinity, and Fullness. Many sections of the *Dao De Jing* are obviously advice about how to rule a country, and this political orientation seems at odds with the contemplative "mysticism" many see in the book, with its advice to "do nothing," with its skepticism about value judgments, and finally with the alienation from conventional society and values expressed in many passages. Some think in fact that the *Dao De Jing* was probably written in at least two stages: first as an apolitical, "mystical" book, advocating withdrawal from public life to contemplate the transcendent Dao; at a later stage someone added the "political" material, applying some of the mystical values to problems of political leadership.

My own recent research[4] into the question of the *Dao De Jing*'s origin suggests that it consists mainly of sayings from the oral tradition of the "Laoists," a Warring States *shi* school, coined probably by several anonymous Laoist teachers, and artfully arranged by teachers in eighty-one "sayings collages" that make up our present book. It was not originally addressed to the general public, but to members of the Laoist school itself, who would have been already familiar with the meaning of its many enigmatic sayings.

Like some of the *shi* described by the *Zhuangzi*, Laoists were alienated from conventional society of their time. This alienation is expressed in the many anticonventional sayings,

like "elegant words are not sincere" (i.e. speakers whom the public greatly admires are typically untrustworthy). Feeling alienated from society, Laoists developed an internal source of personal nourishment, a spirituality centered on cultivating certain states of mind, described by terms like Stillness, Emptiness, Softness, Femininity, Steadiness, Clarity, and Harmony. The terms "Dao" and "De" (*Tao* and *Te*) also refer to the state of mind that Laoists cultivated. Dao and De were conceived of as "cosmic" forces because of the immense foundational importance this state of mind was felt to have in the lives of Laoists.

However, unlike some other Daoists, their alienation and spiritual orientation did not lead Laoists to abandon society and politics for life in the wilderness. They had great ambitions to replace the Emperor as *spiritual* leaders of China, and to exercise this leadership through the traditional middle-level positions held by *shi* as administrators and advisors to rulers. Although many sayings in the *Dao De Jing* are relevant to people in all walks of life, it addresses particularly the problems, opportunities, and especially the *vices* typical of people in positions of authority. It is best seen as an internal critique of *shi* by *shi*, to elevate their attitudes and practice by uncompromising criticism of all the main vices to which people in their position are tempted.

For example, those actively engaged in practical affairs are prone to anxiety, stress, and overstimulation, wearing themselves out. To combat this, the *Dao De Jing* joins those the *Zhuangzi* calls "the nurturers of the body" in advocating meditative exercises that conserve one's life-energy and engender an unshakable internal state of Stillness and Steadiness, immune from the ups and downs of political fortune (see pp. 36, 44, 51–52). Some *shi*, according to the *Zhuangzi*, tended toward ambitious egotism, eager to "talk of great achievements and establish great reputations." Many sayings in the *Dao De Jing* speak directly against this kind of egotistic self-promotion; a good *shi* devotes himself to public service but is self-effacing about his own achievements (see pp. 39, 40–43, 59–60, 95–96).

Some idealistic *shi* of the Confucian persuasion tried to prepare themselves for a role in reformist politics by polishing their own characters, reshaping them according to high notions of Benevolence and Uprightness. The *Dao De Jing* sees these "virtues" as artificial substitutes for a more natural goodness which the *shi* ought to cultivate instead (see pp. 55–56, 68–69, 77). People in charge often see themselves as "knowledge-experts," with a thorough understanding of reality and public affairs, able to articulate this knowledge very clearly in doctrines and laws about the way things are, and able to "work on the world," reshaping it the way it ought to be. Against this, the *Dao De Jing* asserts the inability of *conceptual* knowledge to grasp the real "right Way" (Dao) in which things ought to be done. The truth about the world and how to manage it can only be intuitively understood by one who cultivates depth in his own mind. The *Dao De Jing* also emphasizes the unpredictability of events in the real world, and recommends respecting the spontaneous organic order of the social world—*wu-wei*, "not working"—rather than trying to "work it over" according to some ideal plan (see pp. 32–35, 77).

Those in positions of responsibility often try to win the respect of those under them by awing them, and assertively insisting on recognition of their high status. Against this, the *Dao De Jing* insists that the best ruler is like the ocean, which becomes the greatest of all bodies of water by being lower than all the rivers. Just as all rivers naturally flow toward the "low" ocean, so the allegiance of all the people will flow in a natural and unforced way toward the ruler who presents himself as someone "lower" than they (see pp. 86, 87). Political leaders are often tempted to rely on physical violence to gain and maintain power. Against this, the *Dao De Jing* recommends defeating one's opposition by indirect "soft" measures (this is the origin of Japanese "Judo," from Chinese *rou dao*, literally "soft Tao"), resorting to war only as a last resort (see pp. 61–62, 65–66). Finally, many Warring States *shi* were recommending that the rulers of states should gear up for economic progress by replacing the traditional ways of peasant farmers, encouraging instead personal ambition and calculating rationality as ways of increasing material prosperity. Against this, the *Dao De Jing* was profoundly "conservative," opposing this disturbing "progress" and competitiveness in defense of a simpler, contented agricultural peasant society (see pp. 34–35, 83–84).

Although the *Dao De Jing* was probably written originally by and for the members of a small *shi* school, it very soon became known and influential outside this group. It was declared a *jing*, "authoritative scripture," by the Han dynasty Empress Tou (151–41 B.C.). In the Han Dynasty also, Laozi became associated with a legendary ancient called Huang Di ("Yellow Emperor"). Many influential leaders of this era styled themselves followers of the "Huang-Lao" school of statecraft, which took the *Dao De Jing* as one of its main manuals. Although there was at times a strong rivalry between Daoism and Confucianism, many Confucian scholars throughout Chinese history continued to study and write commentaries on the *Dao De Jing,* and to incorporate its advice both in their self-cultivation and their political practice.

In the late Han period, several religious organizations arose claiming Taoist inspiration, and looking to the *Dao De Jing* as their main "sacred scripture." In later numerous branches of religious Daoism, Laozi was deified and worshiped as Tai Shang Lao Jun ("The Most Exalted Venerable Lord"), and both he and the *Dao De Jing* came to be regarded as visible manifestations of the invisible transcendent Dao. (The legend of Laozi leaving China was also elaborated on, so that his Western journey took him to India where he was known as Gautama the Buddha, teaching the Indians profound Chinese wisdom.) The *Dao De Jing* became a favorite text especially for the many groups who engaged in esoteric meditation practices, who also influenced the practice of both medicine and the martial arts in China.

The first Western translation of the *Dao De Jing* was made by Jesuit missionaries in China in the late 1700s, and was introduced at a meeting of the Royal Society in England in 1788. It has become increasingly popular in many Western countries, especially in the twentieth century. Its popularity, together with its enigmatic style, have attracted scores of translators, making it (along with the Bible and the Bhagavad Gita) one of the most often translated books in world literature. Well over a hundred English translations have appeared, and the trend is growing—by my informal count there have been eight new English translations in the last six years alone.[5] Mr. Tsai Chih Chung's aptly whimsical illustrations of the thoughts of the *Dao De Jing* should bring it to an even wider audience.

Michael LaFargue is Lecturer in Religion and East Asian Studies at the University of Massachusetts, Boston.

Notes

1. I refer to the two new manuscripts of the *Dao De Jing* uncovered in a gravesite at Mawangdui (in China's Hunan province). They date from about 200 B.C., making them by far the oldest extant manuscripts. These manuscripts are introduced and translated in Robert Henrick's *Lao-Tzu: Te-Tao Ching: A New Translation Based on the Recently Discovered Ma-wang-tui Texts* (New York: Ballantine, 1989).

2. Cho-yun Hsu's *Ancient China in Transition: An analysis of social mobility, 722–22* (Stanford: Stanford University Press, 1965) gives an excellent and detailed picture of the political, economic, and socio-cultural trends in the Warring States period. See especially pp. 34–37, 89–106, on the rise in importance of the *shi* (shih).

3. For the intellectual history of the period see the recent surveys by two leading scholars, Benjamin Schwartz (*The World of Thought in Ancient China.* Cambridge: Harvard Univ. Pr. 1985) and A. C. Graham (*Disputers of the Tao: Philosophical Argument in Ancient China.* LaSalle, Ill.: Open Court, 1990).

4. The results of my research are given in *The Tao of the Dao De Jing: A Translation and Commentary* (Albany, New York: SUNY Press, 1992); a more comprehensive presentation of evidence and argumentation is given in *Tao and Method: A Reasoned Approach to the Dao De Jing* (Albany, New York: SUNY Press, 1994).

5. Among the best translations by knowledgeable scholars are those of Arthur Waley, D. C. Lau, J. J. L. Duyvendak, Wing-Tsit Chan, and the joint translation by Stephen Addiss and Stanley Lombardo. For those wanting a very literal translation, Yi Wu's *The Book of Lao Tzu* (San Francisco: Great Learning Publishing Co., 1989) gives the Chinese text with English equivalents next to each Chinese character.

THE WISDOM OF LIFE

FROM THE MOST ANCIENT TIMES, THE STANDARD TEACHINGS HAD BEEN:

YOU MUST EXHIBIT YOUR STRENGTH AND INTELLIGENCE; DON'T LET PEOPLE THINK YOU ARE WEAK OR FOOLISH.

HOWEVER, A VERY UNIQUE MAN NAMED LAOZI APPEARED EARLY ON IN CHINESE HISTORY.

EXHIBIT WEAKNESS AND FOOLISHNESS; DON'T LET PEOPLE THINK YOU ARE STRONG OR INTELLIGENT. REMEMBER THE IMPORTANCE OF NON-ACTION, NO-SELF, NO-DESIRES, HUMILITY, TRANQUILLITY, BEING NATURAL . . .

MOST PEOPLE THINK THAT BEING STRONG IS GOOD!

BUT STRENGTH WILL BREAK WHERE WEAKNESS WILL REMAIN INTACT.

老子者，楚苦縣厲鄉曲仁里人也，姓李氏，名耳、字聃、周守藏室之史也。

孔子適周，將問禮於老子。老子曰：「子所言者，其人與骨皆已朽矣，獨其言在耳。且君子得其時則駕，不得其時則蓬累而行。吾聞之，良賈深藏若虛，君子盛德容貌若愚。去子之驕氣與多欲，態色與淫志，是皆無益於子之身。吾所以告子，若是而已。」孔子去，謂弟子曰：「鳥，吾知其能飛；魚，吾知其能游

17

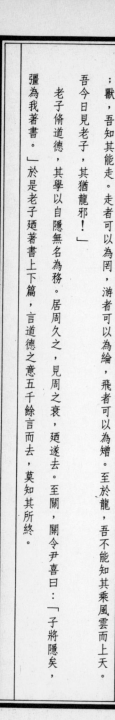

；獸，吾知其能走。走者可以為罔，游者可以為綸，飛者可以為矰。至於龍，吾不能知其乘風雲而上天。

吾今日見老子，其猶龍邪！」

老子脩道德，其學以自隱無名為務。居周久之，見周之衰，迺遂去。至關，關令尹喜曰：「子將隱矣，彊為我著書。」於是老子迺著書上下篇，言道德之意五千餘言而去，莫知其所終。

自孔子死之後百二十九年，而史記周太史儋見秦獻公曰「始秦與周合，合五百歲而離，離七十歲而霸王者出焉。」或曰儋即老子；或曰非也，世莫知其然否。老子，隱君子也。

老子之子名宗，宗為魏將，封於段干。宗子注，注子宮，宮玄孫假，假仕於漢孝文帝。而假之子解為膠西王卬太傅，因家于齊焉。

世之學老子者則絀儒學，儒學亦絀老子。「道不同不相為謀」，豈謂是邪？李耳無為自化，清靜自正。

IS NOT LAOZI LIKE THE DRAGON!

ABOUT TWENTY-FIVE CENTURIES AGO, SOPHISTICATED CULTURES FLOURISHED IN SEVERAL PARTS OF THE WORLD. THESE CULTURES BROUGHT FORTH OUTSTANDING SCHOLARS AND THINKERS. IN GREECE, THERE WERE THE GREAT PHILOSOPHERS THALES AND HERACLITUS.

IN INDIA, SIDDHĀRTHA GAUTAMA FOUNDED THE BUDDHIST RELIGION.

OF THESE, THE MOST INFLUENTIAL WERE THE CONFUCIANISTS, DAOISTS, MOISTS, AND LEGALISTS. A GREAT COMMUNICATOR OF WHAT CAME TO BE KNOWN AS THE DAOIST SCHOOL WAS A MAN WE CALL LAOZI.

IN CHINA, DURING THE SPRING & AUTUMN AND WARRING STATES PERIODS (770-221 B.C.), NUMEROUS SCHOOLS OF THOUGHT AROSE AND COMPETED VIGOROUSLY FOR DOMINATION.

YIN YANG
NAMES
MISCELLANEOUS
CONFUCIANISM
AGRICULTURISTS
MOISM
DIPLOMATISTS
LEGALISM
DAOISM

現在一般通行的老子書，都分上下篇。上篇的第一句是「道可道，非常道。」下篇的第一句是「上德不德，是以有德。」因此後人就取上篇的「道」字和下篇的「德」字，合起來稱它為「道德經」……。

史記老子傳說：「老子迺著書上下篇，言道德之意五千餘言。」這和現行的道德經符合。

21

ACCORDING TO CERTAIN HISTORICAL RECORDS, LAOZI'S SURNAME WAS LI, HIS GIVEN NAME ER, AND HIS COMING-OF-AGE NAME DAN. HE WAS BORN IN THE SIXTH CENTURY B.C. IN QUREN VILLAGE, LI DISTRICT, HU COUNTY, IN THE STATE OF CHU.

LEGEND HAS IT THAT HE WAS APPOINTED CARETAKER OF THE STATE ARCHIVES UNDER KING WU OF ZHOU IN THE ZHOU CAPITAL OF LUOYANG.

I'D LIKE TO BORROW TWO BOOKS, PLEASE.

OK, SIGN RIGHT HERE.

HERE, LAOZI PORED THROUGH INNUMERABLE BOOKS, ABSORBING THE KNOWLEDGE OF THE TIMES AND GAINING MANY INSIGHTS INTO LIFE.

AND IN THIS WAY, LAOZI GREW WISER BY THE DAY.

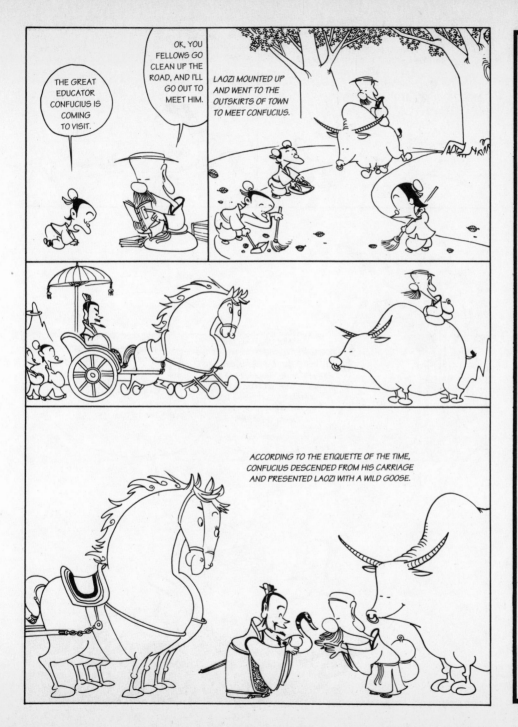

老子是楚國人，楚國位居中國的南方，這一點對他的思想有非常大的影響。因為南方風氣柔弱，不像北方風氣剛強，因此形成老子重視柔弱的思想。在禮記中庸裡，孔子就曾說過：「寬柔以教，不報無道，南方之強也。衽金革，死而不厭，北方之強也。」……。

我們看老子一再講「守柔曰強」（五十二章）「柔弱勝剛強」（三十六章）「強梁者不得其死」（四十二章）這不是「寬柔以教」嗎？老子又說：「報怨以德」（六十三章）這不是「不報無道」嗎？

23

老子所處的時代是春秋的晚期。這時候齊桓、晉文的霸業早已過去，而由南方蠻夷國吳越爭霸。

老子雖和孔子處在同一時代，但是由於出身不同，地域各異，所以應付的方法也就不同。政治方面，他主張「無為」，贊成治政者「無心，以百姓心為心」(四十九章)的民主。軍事方面，他反對戰爭，他認為「兵者，不祥之器，物或惡之，故有道者不處。」(三十章)社會倫理方面，他反對禮制，說「禮者，忠信之薄，而亂之始也」(三十八章)

24

史記老子傳說老子曾做過周室的柱下史，這個職務，相當於現在的圖書館的館長。由於職務上的便利，他可以飽覽羣書，對歷史上的成敗、存亡、禍福，看的多了，知道世界上的一切紛爭都是起於欲念，一切罪惡都是肇因於人為，所以他主張歸真返樸，致虛守靜，棄人事而任自然。班固漢書藝文志諸子略序說道家：「知秉要執本，清虛以自守，卑弱以自持。」真是一針見血。

依據史記的記載，老子活了一百六十多歲，這很有可能。因為老子修道養壽，年壽當然比一般人高，他的名字叫「聃」，說文：「聃，耳曼也。」「耳曼」就是耳長，耳長又是長壽的特徵。……史記說老子「居關久之，見周之衰，迺遂去。」那麼，老子在寫書的時候，至少也有七十歲左右，當然對世事物理，能夠看得透透徹徹，再加上深厚的學養，自然能形成玄妙而有系統的思想了。

BOOK 1:

THE WAY

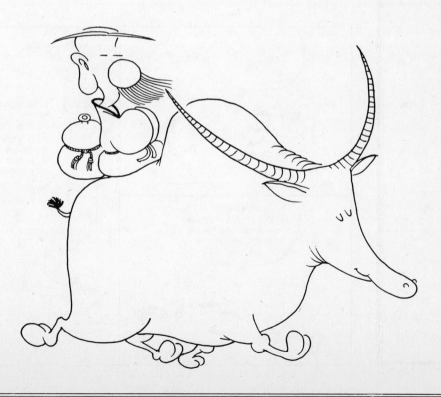

● 道可道，非常『道』：第一個『道』字和第三個『道』字，是老子哲學上的專有名詞，在本章它意指構成宇宙的實體與動力。第二個『道』字，是指言說的意思。

● 名可名，非常『名』：第一個『名』字和第三個『名』字為老子特用術語，是稱『道』之名。文法上屬於名詞使用。第二個『名』字是稱謂的意思，作動詞使用。

THE DAO
THAT
CAN'T BE
SPOKEN

THE DAO IS LIKE THIS, IT DOES THIS, AND IT ISN'T THIS . . .

OH, I GET IT!

EXCUSE ME, BUT I BELIEVE YOU ARE MISTAKEN. IF YOU CAN EXPLAIN THE DAO CLEARLY, THEN THAT IS NOT THE DAO.

THE DAO ENCOMPASSES THE PRINCIPLES OF THE MYRIAD THINGS. IT IS FORMLESS, SILENT, HAS NO BODY, AND IS ETERNAL AND UNCHANGING. THIS PRINCIPLE CANNOT BE CLEARLY EXPLAINED THROUGH LANGUAGE.

『無』，名天地之使；『有』，名萬物之母：『無』是天地的本始，『有』是萬物的根源。『無』、『有』是指稱『道』的，是表明『道』由無形質落實向有形質的活動過程。

◎ 常『無』欲以觀其妙，常『有』欲以觀其徼：常體『無』，以觀照『道』的奧妙；常體『有』，以觀照『道』的邊際。

◎ 此兩者：指『無』和『有』。

29

● 玄：幽昧深遠的意思。

● 眾妙之門：一切變化的總門，即指『道』而言。

NOTHING AND BEING—ONE IS THE SUBSTANCE, AND THE OTHER IS THE FUNCTION. YOU CAN SAY THEY BOTH COME FROM THE DAO, THEY JUST HAVE DIFFERENT NAMES IS ALL!

NOTHING

BEING

THEY CAN BOTH BE CALLED MYSTERIOUS, EVEN MORE MYSTERIOUS THAN MYSTERIOUS!

YES, THAT'S THE DAO, THE SOURCE OF CREATION FOR THE UNIVERSE AND THE MYRIAD THINGS.

DAO

THE UNDERLYING SUBSTANCE OF THE UNIVERSE IS NOTHINGNESS. FROM NOTHING CAME HEAVEN AND EARTH. FROM HEAVEN AND EARTH CAME THE MYRIAD THINGS, FINALLY GIVING RISE TO THE WORLD AS WE KNOW IT.

『道』是老子哲學上的一個中心觀念，在老子書上它含有幾種意義：(1)構成世界的實體。(2)創造宇宙的動力。(3)促使萬物運動的規律。(4)作為人類行為的準則。本章所說的『道』，是指一切存在的根源，是自然界中最初的發動者。它具有無限的潛在力和創造力，天地間萬物蓬勃的生長都是『道』的潛藏力之不斷創發的一種表現。

●『聖人』：這是道家最高的理想人物，其人格形態

●音聲相和：樂器的音響和人的聲音互相調和。

●天下皆知美之為美，斯惡已：天下都知道美之所以為美，醜的認識產生了。

，不同於儒家；儒家的聖人是典範化的道德人，道家的『聖人』則體任自然，拓展內在的生命，以「虛靜」「不爭」為理想的生活，卑棄名教，揚棄一切影響身心自由活動的束縛（甚至包括倫常規範

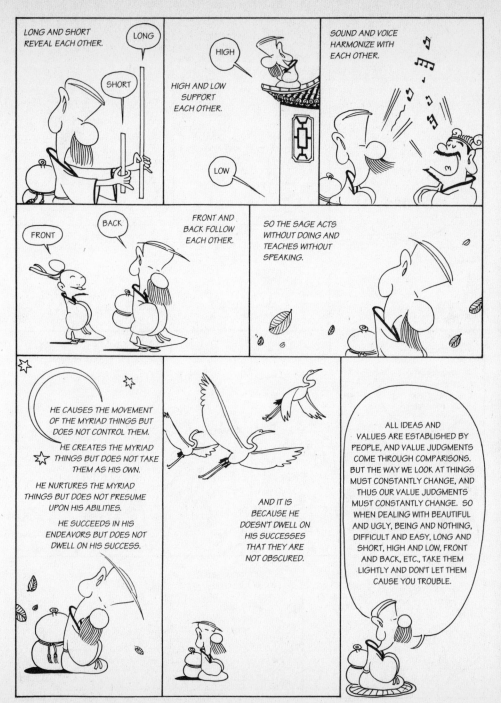

在內。)

◎無為：順其自然，不妄為。

◉不言：不發號施令，不用政令。「言」，指政教號令。「不言之教」，意指非形式條規的督教，而為

潛移默化的引導。

◉尚賢：標榜賢名。

◉不爭：不爭功名，返自然也。

◉虛其心：清淨人民的心思。

◉弱其志：減損人民的志意。

◉無知無欲：沒有偽詐的心智，沒有爭盜的欲念。

◉智者不敢為也：自作聰明的人不敢多事。

◉為「無為」：以「無為」（順任自然而不強作妄為）的態度去處理事務。

BY NOT PLACING VALUE ON THINGS DIFFICULT TO OBTAIN, YOU CAN KEEP PEOPLE FROM WANTING TO STEAL THINGS.

BY NOT REWARDING FAME, YOU CAN KEEP PEOPLE FROM MUDDLING THEIR MINDS WITH IT.

FAME

SO A SAGE GOVERNS BY PURIFYING THE HEARTS OF THE PEOPLE. HE KEEPS PEOPLE SECURE AND SATISFIED, ELIMINATES THEIR SCHEMING AMBITIONS, AND STRENGTHENS THEIR BODIES.

HE CAUSES THE PEOPLE TO HAVE NO DECEPTIVE KNOWLEDGE OR COVETOUS DESIRES. HE CAUSES THE CUNNING ONES TO REFRAIN FROM ENGAGING IN UNSAVORY ACTS.

BY ACTING IN ACCORDANCE WITH NATURE AND GOVERNING SELFLESSLY, THERE WILL BE NOTHING IN THE COUNTRY THAT IS NOT WELL-GOVERNED.

FAME AND POSITION INCITE CONTENTION, WEALTH EXCITES PEOPLE'S GREED. AS A RESULT, LYING AND DECEIT ARISE IN ENDLESS SUCCESSION, AND THESE LEAD TO CONFUSION AND CONFLICTS IN SOCIETY.

名位實足以引起人的爭逐，財貨實足以激起人的貪圖。名位的爭逐，財貨的貪圖，於是巧詐偽作的心智活動就層出不窮了，這是導致社會的混亂與衝突的主要原因。解決的方法，一方面要給人民適度的安飽，另一方面要淨化他們貪圖的心念，削減他們攘奪的心機。所謂「無知」，並不是行愚民政策，乃是消解巧偽的心智。所謂「無欲」，並不是要滅除自然的本能，而是消解貪欲的擴張。

35

◉ 天地不仁：天地無所偏愛。即意指天地只是個物理的、自然的存在，並不具有人類般的感情；萬物在天地間僅依循著自然的法則運行著，並不像有神論所想像的，以為天地自然法則對某物有所愛顧（或對某物有所嫌棄），其實這只是人類感情的投射作用罷了！

◉ 芻狗：用草紮成的狗，作為祭祀時使用。

◉ 聖人不仁：「聖人」無所偏愛。即意指「聖人」取法

37

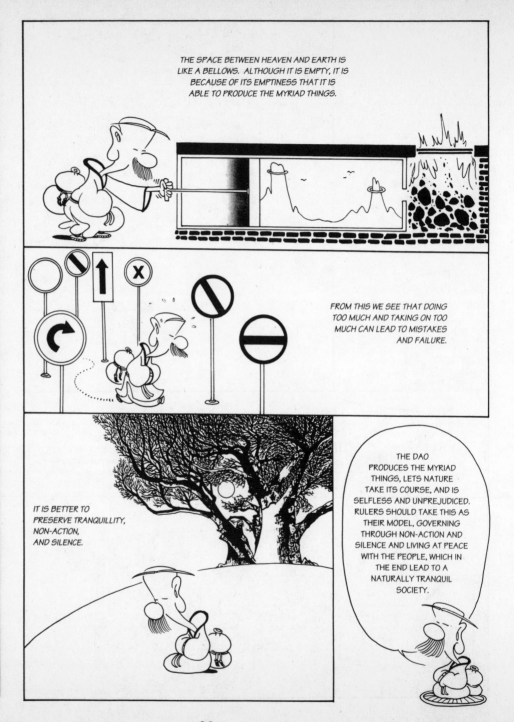

於天地之純任自然。
● 樂籥：風箱。
● 不屈：不竭。
● 多言數窮：政令煩苛，加速敗亡。「言」，意指聲

教法令。「多言」，意指政令煩多。「數」，通「速」。

● 守中：作「守冲」解。持守虛靜的意思。

38

OUR WORLD ETERNAL

HEAVEN AND EARTH ARE EVERLASTING BECAUSE THEY DO NOT EXIST FOR THEMSELVES.

IN ALL HE DOES, A SAGE IS MODEST AND YIELDS TO OTHERS, AND AS A RESULT, HE WINS THE ADORATION OF OTHERS.

HE GIVES NO THOUGHT TO PROFIT AND LOSS, AND YET IS BENEFITED BY THIS.

BECAUSE HE IS UNSELFISH, HE ENDS UP ACHIEVING WHAT IS IN HIS OWN BEST INTEREST.

MODESTY WINS ADORATION. BY DOING THINGS FOR OTHERS, YOU CAN ACCOMPLISH YOUR OWN IDEALS.

●以其不自生：指天地的運作不為自己。

●長生：長久。

●後其身而身先：把自己放在後面，反而能得到大家的愛戴。

●成其私：成就他自己。

39

● 上善若水：「上善之人，如水之性。」

● 幾：近。

● 淵：形容沉靜。

● 與善仁：「與」，指和別人相交相接。

● 正善治：為政於善完成良好的治績。

● 尤：怨咎。

VIRTUE RESEMBLES WATER

A VIRTUOUS PERSON IS LIKE WATER.

WATER HAS THREE SPECIAL CHARACTERISTICS: ONE, IT NURTURES THE MYRIAD THINGS.

TWO, IT IS NATURALLY PLIANT—FLOWING WHERE NATURE TAKES IT.

THREE, IT RESIDES IN LOWLY PLACES DESPISED BY PEOPLE.

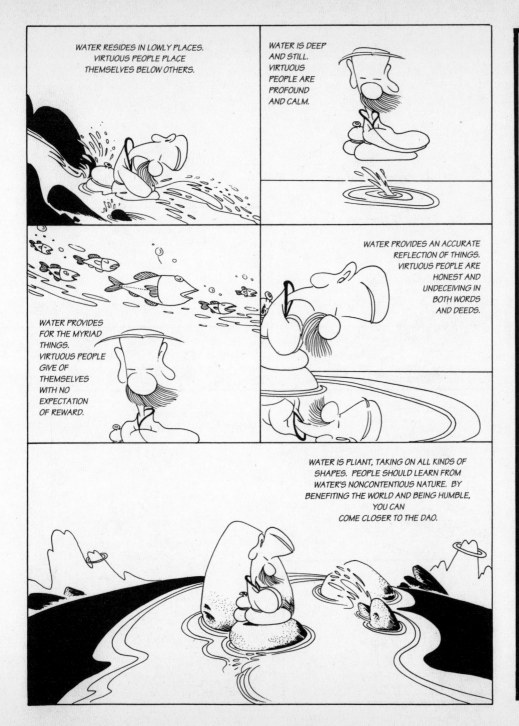

WATER RESIDES IN LOWLY PLACES. VIRTUOUS PEOPLE PLACE THEMSELVES BELOW OTHERS.

WATER IS DEEP AND STILL. VIRTUOUS PEOPLE ARE PROFOUND AND CALM.

WATER PROVIDES FOR THE MYRIAD THINGS. VIRTUOUS PEOPLE GIVE OF THEMSELVES WITH NO EXPECTATION OF REWARD.

WATER PROVIDES AN ACCURATE REFLECTION OF THINGS. VIRTUOUS PEOPLE ARE HONEST AND UNDECEIVING IN BOTH WORDS AND DEEDS.

WATER IS PLIANT, TAKING ON ALL KINDS OF SHAPES. PEOPLE SHOULD LEARN FROM WATER'S NONCONTENTIOUS NATURE. BY BENEFITING THE WORLD AND BEING HUMBLE, YOU CAN COME CLOSER TO THE DAO.

本章用水性來比喻上德者的人格。水最顯著的特性和作用是：㈠柔。㈡停留在卑下的地方。㈢滋潤萬物而不與相爭。老子認為最完善的人格也應具有這種心態與行為：「處衆人之所惡。」別人不願去的地方，他願意去；別人不願意做的事，他願意做。他具有駱駝般的精神，堅忍負重，居卑忍辱。他能盡其所能地去貢獻自己的力量以幫助別人，而絕不和別人爭功爭名爭利，這就是老子「善利萬物而不爭」的思想。

41

●持而盈之：執持盈滿，含有自滿自驕的意思。
●已：止。
●揣而銳之：捶擊使它尖銳，含有顯露鋒芒的意思。
●功遂：功業成就。
●身退：指斂藏鋒芒。
●天之道：指自然的規律。

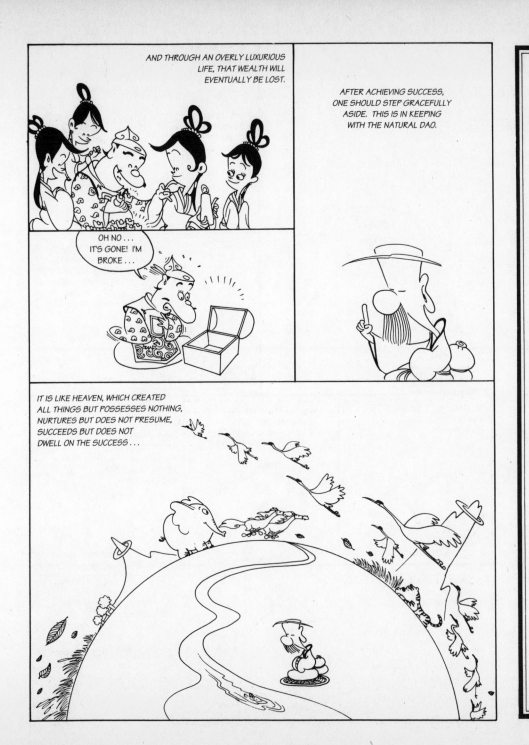

AND THROUGH AN OVERLY LUXURIOUS LIFE, THAT WEALTH WILL EVENTUALLY BE LOST.

AFTER ACHIEVING SUCCESS, ONE SHOULD STEP GRACEFULLY ASIDE. THIS IS IN KEEPING WITH THE NATURAL DAO.

OH NO... IT'S GONE! I'M BROKE...

IT IS LIKE HEAVEN, WHICH CREATED ALL THINGS BUT POSSESSES NOTHING, NURTURES BUT DOES NOT PRESUME, SUCCEEDS BUT DOES NOT DWELL ON THE SUCCESS...

本章在於寫「盈」。「盈」即是滿溢、過度的意思。自滿自驕，都是「盈」的表現。持「盈」的結果，將不免於傾覆之患。所以老子諄諄告誡人不可「盈」，一個人在功成名就之後，如能「身退」不盈，才是長保之道。「身退」並不是引身而去，更不是隱匿形跡。王真說：「身退者，非謂必使其功成而不有之耳」。「身退」即是斂藏，不發露。老子要人在完成功業之後，不把恃，不據有，不露鋒芒，不咄咄逼人。可見老子所說的「身退」，並不是要人做隱士，只是要人不膨脹自我。

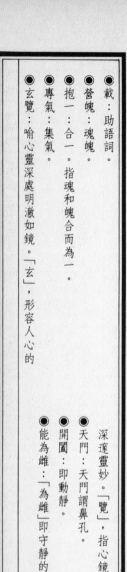

◉載：助語詞。
◉營魄：魂魄。
◉抱一：合一。指魂和魄合而為一。
◉專氣：集氣。
◉玄覽：喻心靈深處明澈如鏡。「玄」，形容人心的深邃靈妙。「覽」，指心鏡的觀照。
◉天門：天門謂鼻孔。
◉開闔：即動靜。
◉能為雌：「為雌」即守靜的意思。

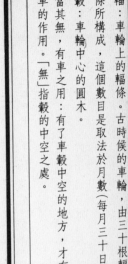

◎輻：車輪上的輻條。古時候的車輪，由三十根輻條所構成，這個數目是取法於月數（每月三十日）。

◎轂：車輪中心的圓木。

◎當其無，有車之用：有了車轂中空的地方，才有車的作用。「無」指轂的中空之處。

◎埏埴：埏，和。埴，陶土。和土做成飲食的器皿。

◎戶牖：門窗。

◎有之以為利，無之以為用：「有」給人便利，「無」發揮了它的作用。

老子舉了三個例子：車的作用在於運貨載人，器皿的作用在於盛物，室的作用在於居住。這是車、器、室給人的便利，所以說：「有之以為利。」然而，如果車子沒有轂輞中空的地方可以轉軸，就無法行駛；器皿如果沒有中間空虛的地方，就無法盛物；室屋如果沒有四壁門窗中空的地方可以出入通明，就無法居住。可見得中空的地方所發揮的作用了，所以說：「無之以為用。」

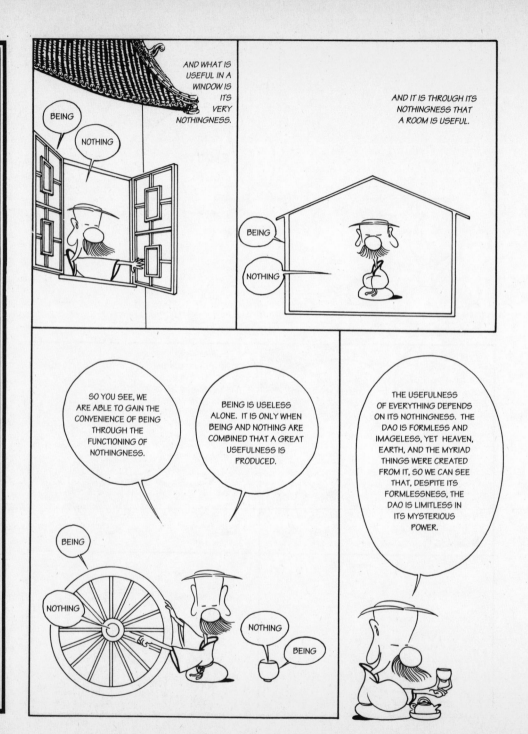

46

BOUNDLESS DESIRES

PEOPLE'S NEEDS HAVE LIMITS, YET OUR DESIRES ARE BOUNDLESS.

OVERINDULGING IN THE SENSE OF SIGHT WILL LEAD TO WEARY EYES.

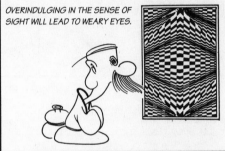

OVERINDULGING IN THE SENSE OF HEARING WILL LEAD TO HEARING LOSS.

BONG

IT'S TOO NOISY, I CAN'T HEAR!

◉五色：指青、赤、黄、白、黑。

◉目盲：喻眼花撩亂。

◉五音：指角、徵、宮、商、羽。

◉耳聾：喻聽覺不露。

◉五味：指酸、苦、甘、辛、鹹。

◉口爽：口病。「爽」，引申為傷，亡。喻味覺差失。

◉馳騁：縱橫奔走，喻縱情。

◉畋：獵取禽獸。

47

● 心發狂：心放蕩而不可制止。

● 行妨：傷害操行。「妨」，害，傷。

● 為腹不為目：只求安飽，不求縱情於聲色之娛。

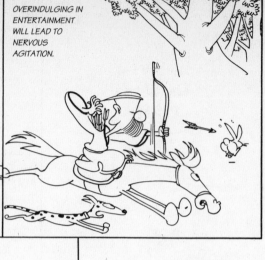

OVERINDULGING IN THE SENSE OF TASTE WILL LEAD TO A LOSS OF APPETITE.

OVERINDULGING IN ENTERTAINMENT WILL LEAD TO NERVOUS AGITATION.

OVERZEALOUSLY PURSUING WEALTH WILL LEAD TO INJURY OF YOUR MORAL CHARACTER AND REPUTATION.

THEREFORE, THE SAGE WHO UNDERSTANDS THE DAO LIVES A SIMPLE LIFE, EATING ONLY UNTIL FULL AND NOT PURSUING SENSUAL PLEASURES. HE IS SATISFIED WITH A QUIET LIFE AND NOT CONCERNED WITH LUXURY AND SPLENDOR.

"THE SEA OF DESIRES IS DIFFICULT TO STAY"—IF YOU CANNOT RID YOURSELF OF DESIRES, YOU WILL SURELY DROWN. A PERSON WITH UNCONTROLLABLE DESIRES WILL NOT ONLY BE UNABLE TO FEEL SATISFIED OR COMFORTABLE, BUT CONVERSELY, WILL FEEL PAIN AND WILL HARM HIS SENSE OF SELF.

HONOR'S DISGRACE

BECAUSE PEOPLE ARE TOO CONCERNED WITH FAME AND FORTUNE, THEY ARE ALWAYS APPREHENSIVE ABOUT BEING HONORED OR DISGRACED.

HONOR

DISGRACE

IT IS BECAUSE PEOPLE BELIEVE HONOR IS SOMETHING TO BE PRIZED, THAT WINNING THE RESPECT OF OTHERS IS THE NOBLEST OF THINGS. IT IS ON ACCOUNT OF THIS THAT THEY ARE TERRIFIED OF LOSING THEIR HONOR.

THEY CONSTANTLY FEAR DISASTER AND HARM THEMSELVES BY THIS. WHAT IS THE REASON?

●寵辱若驚：得寵和受辱都使人驚慌。
●貴大患若身：重視身體一如重視大患。「貴」，重視。「身」，身體。
●寵為下：得寵是不光容的。「下」即卑下的意思。

●吾所以有大患者，為吾有身，及吾無身，吾有何患：這是說大患是來自身體，所以防大患，應先貴身。老子說這話是含有警惕的意思，並不是要人棄身或忘身。

49

DISGRACE IS SHAMEFUL AND EMBARRASSING, AND IS THEREFORE TO BE FEARED.

THE REASON WE HAVE DISASTERS OF THIS KIND IS THAT WE WORRY TOO MUCH ABOUT OURSELVES...

IF WE CAN FORGET ABOUT THE "SELF," WHAT IS THERE LEFT TO WORRY ABOUT?

THEREFORE, IF A PERSON IS WILLING TO SACRIFICE HIMSELF FOR THE WORLD, THEN THAT PERSON IS WORTHY OF BEING ENTRUSTED WITH THE WORLD.

PEOPLE SHOULD BE UNSELFISH AND SELF-FORGETTING. IF YOU CAN SET LIFE AND DEATH ASIDE, AND IF YOU ARE UNMOVED BY HONOR AND DISGRACE, FORTUNE AND MISFORTUNE, THEN IS THERE REALLY ANYTHING LEFT TO BE AFRAID OF?

MAINTAINING TRANQUILLITY

PEOPLE'S SOULS ARE ORIGINALLY VACUOUS AND TRANQUIL.

BUT SOMEHOW WE ARE ALWAYS BLINDED BY SELFISH DESIRE.

AS A RESULT, WE CANNOT VIEW THINGS CLEARLY, AND OUR ACTIONS LOSE THEIR CONSTANCY.

JADE!

THUS, WE MUST TRY TO RETURN TO A STATE OF VACUITY AND TRANQUILLITY. THIS WAY, WE CAN WITNESS THE FLOURISHING OF THE MYRIAD THINGS AND SEE THE RECURRENT CYCLES OF THE NATURAL PROCESS.

● 致虛極，守靜篤：「虛」「靜」形容心境原本是空明寧靜的狀態，只因私慾的活動與外界的擾動，而使得心靈蔽塞不安，所以必須時時做「致虛」「守靜」的工夫，以恢復心靈的清明。

● 作：生成活動。

● 復：返，往復循環。

● 芸芸：紛雜茂盛。芸芸，常用來形容草木的繁盛。

● 歸根：回歸原本。

51

◉ 復命：復歸本性。

◉ 常：指萬物運動與變化中的不變之律則。

◉ 明：萬物的運動和變化都依循着循環往復的律則，對於這種律則的認識和了解，叫做「明」。

◉ 容：寬容，包容。

◉ 全：周徧。

◉ 天：指自然的天，或為自然的代稱。

THE MYRIAD THINGS ARE MANY AND VARIED, AND EVENTUALLY EACH ONE RETURNS TO ITS SOURCE. THIS IS CALLED "TRANQUILLITY." IT IS ALSO CALLED "CONSTANCY." UNDERSTANDING CONSTANCY IS CALLED "ENLIGHTENMENT." THOSE WHO DO NOT UNDERSTAND CONSTANCY AND ARE RASH AND IMPULSIVE WILL EVENTUALLY ENCOUNTER GREAT TROUBLE.

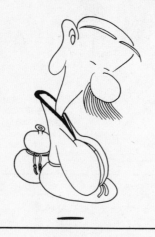

ONE WHO UNDERSTANDS THE "CONSTANT DAO" IS ALL-ENCOMPASSING; BEING ALL-ENCOMPASSING, ONE IS OPEN AND JUST; BEING OPEN AND JUST, ONE IS UNIVERSAL; BEING UNIVERSAL, ONE IS IN ACCORD WITH NATURE; BEING IN ACCORD WITH NATURE, ONE IS IN ACCORD WITH THE DAO.

BY BEING IN ACCORD WITH THE DAO, WE GAIN LONGEVITY, AND LONGEVITY MEANS A LIFE FREE FROM DANGER.

THROUGH "ATTAINING VACUITY" AND "MAINTAINING TRANQUILLITY," YOU WILL COME TO CLEARLY EXAMINE THE PRINCIPLES OF THE WORLD AND THOROUGHLY UNDERSTAND THE TRANSFORMATIONS OF THE MYRIAD THINGS. YOU WILL BE ABLE TO PROFOUNDLY APPRECIATE NATURE'S SUBTLETIES AND BECOME ONE WITH THE DAO.

● 不知有之：人民不知道有君主的存在。

● 悠兮：悠閑的樣子。

● 貴言：不輕於發號施令。

● 自然：自己如此。

53

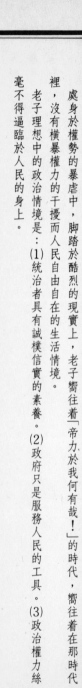

REGRESSION INTO BENEVOLENCE

IN THE EARLY DAYS OF CIVILIZATION, PEOPLE WERE SIMPLE AND HONEST. THEY COULDN'T READ, AND THEY DIDN'T KNOW MUCH, BUT AT THE SAME TIME, THEY WEREN'T GREEDY OR DISHONEST.

I'LL HAVE TO USE MY HEAD TO KEEP HIM FROM EVADING TAXES.

LATER ON IN HISTORY, PEOPLE BECAME MORE AND MORE CUNNING. AS A RESULT, GOVERNMENT LEADERS WERE FORCED TO USE THEIR INTELLIGENCE TO CREATE A LEGAL SYSTEM TO KEEP THE PEOPLE IN LINE.

I'LL HAVE TO USE MY HEAD TO AVOID PAYING TAXES.

THIS IS WHEN HYPOCRISY AND DECEIT AROSE.

ORIGINALLY, FAMILIES WERE HAPPY AND THE MEMBERS GOT ALONG VERY WELL WITH EACH OTHER. THERE WAS NO NEED FOR SUCH CONCEPTS AS "FILIAL PIETY" OR "PARENTAL KINDNESS."

BUT WHEN FAMILY RELATIONSHIPS BEGAN TO BREAK DOWN, CONCEPTS SUCH AS THESE BECAME IMPORTANT.

BE NICE! RESPECT YOUR ELDERS! BE GOOD!

◎ 智慧：智巧。

● 六親：父、子、兄、弟、夫、婦。

魚在水中，不覺得水的重要，不覺得水的重要；人在空氣中，不覺得空氣的重要；大道興隆，仁義行於其中，自然不覺得有倡導仁義的必要。等到崇尚仁義的時代，社會已經是不純厚了。

某種德行的表彰，正由於它特別欠缺的緣故；猶如現在所謂好人好事的表揚，正由於這些事跡極其稀罕的緣故。

WHEN THE COUNTRY WAS STILL PURE AND INNOCENT, GOVERNMENT MINISTERS ALL DID WHAT THEY WERE SUPPOSED TO, AND THERE WAS NO SUCH THING AS A "LOYAL MINISTER."

THEY ARE ALL MY MINISTERS!

BUT WHEN THE COUNTRY FELL INTO CHAOS, AND MINISTERS BEGAN SCHEMING AMONG THEMSELVES, THE WORDS "LOYAL MINISTER" BECAME NECESSARY.

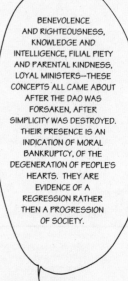

BENEVOLENCE AND RIGHTEOUSNESS, KNOWLEDGE AND INTELLIGENCE, FILIAL PIETY AND PARENTAL KINDNESS, LOYAL MINISTERS—THESE CONCEPTS ALL CAME ABOUT AFTER THE DAO WAS FORSAKEN, AFTER SIMPLICITY WAS DESTROYED. THEIR PRESENCE IS AN INDICATION OF MORAL BANKRUPTCY, OF THE DEGENERATION OF PEOPLE'S HEARTS. THEY ARE EVIDENCE OF A REGRESSION RATHER THEN A PROGRESSION OF SOCIETY.

THIS MAN IS MY ONLY LOYAL MINISTER!

LIVING WITH THE DAO

KNOWLEDGE AND LEARNING ARE THE ROOT CAUSES OF DISTRESS. FORSAKE THEM, AND YOU WILL FREE YOURSELF OF TROUBLE AND WORRY.

PEOPLE SEEK HONOR AND AVOID DISGRACE. THEY REACH FOR GOODNESS AND SHUN BADNESS. BUT IS THERE REALLY SUCH A GREAT DIFFERENCE BETWEEN HONOR AND DISGRACE? BETWEEN HIGH AND LOW? BETWEEN GOOD AND BAD?

NEVERTHELESS, I CAN'T EXIST ENTIRELY ALONE OR MAKE A SHOWY DISPLAY OF MY UNIQUENESS. WHAT OTHER PEOPLE FEAR, I MUST ALSO FEAR.

THE DAO, HOWEVER, IS VAST AND LIMITLESS. OH, WHAT A DIFFERENCE BETWEEN IT AND THE WORLD IN WHICH WE LIVE.

◉絕學無憂：「學」，指仁義聖智禮法之學。

◉唯之與阿：「唯」，恭敬的答應，這是晚輩回應長輩的聲音。「阿」，怠慢的答應，這是長輩回應晚輩的聲音。「唯」、「阿」都是回應的聲音，「阿」的聲音高，「唯」的聲音低，在這裡用以表示上下或

貴賤的區別。

◉熙熙：縱情奔欲，興高彩烈的樣子。

◉荒兮其未央哉：精神包含廣遠而沒有邊際。「荒兮」，廣漠的樣子。「未央」，即無盡的意思。

◉享太牢：參加豐盛的筵席。「享」，作饗。「太牢」

57

THE MASSES LOOK EXCITED AND HAPPY, AS IF THEY WERE ATTENDING A FEAST OR STANDING IN A TOWER IN THE SPRINGTIME LOOKING OUT AT AN EXPANSIVE VIEW.

ONLY I AM AT PEACE IN MY CALM SINCERITY, LIKE AN INFANT THAT HAS NOT YET LEARNED TO SMILE. I APPEAR WEARY, AS IF I WERE HOMELESS!

THE MASSES ALL HAVE MORE THAN ENOUGH, AND ONLY I APPEAR TO BE LACKING. OH, I AM SO FOOLISH, AS IF I WERE MUDDLED AND CONFUSED.

EVERYONE IS SO BRIGHT AND DAZZLING, AND ONLY I APPEAR OBTUSE AND STUPID.

EVERYONE IS SO INTELLIGENT AND TALENTED, AND ONLY I APPEAR COMPLETELY UNDISCERNING.

EVERYONE SEEMS CAPABLE OF DOING SO MUCH, AND ONLY I APPEAR FOOLISH AND INEPT. I AM DIFFERENT FROM THEM—I LIVE WITH THE DAO.

道
DAO

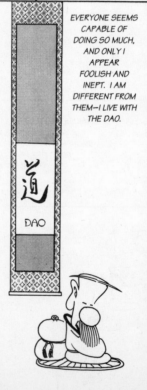

HIGH, LOW; GOOD, BAD; RIGHT, WRONG; BEAUTIFUL, UGLY—THESE ARE MERE VALUE JUDGMENTS RATHER THAN INTRINSIC QUALITIES. THEY ARE RELATIVE AND CHANGE ACCORDING TO THE TIMES AND ENVIRONMENT. PEOPLE INDULGE SO MUCH IN SOUND, SEX, MATERIAL THINGS, AND PROFIT; BUT PERHAPS WE SHOULD BE HAPPY IN TRANQUILLITY, TAKE PLEASURE IN SIMPLICITY, AND SEEK ELEVATION OF THE SPIRIT.

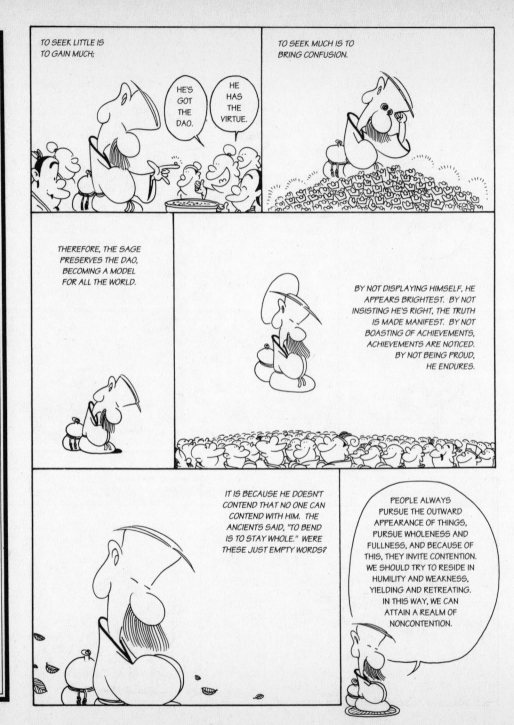

常人總喜歡追逐事物的顯相，芸芸眾生莫不汲汲於求「全」求「盈」，或急急於彰揚顯溢，因而引起的無數爭紛。求全之道，莫過於「不爭」。「不爭」之道，在於「不自見（現）」，「不自是」，「不自我」，「不自矜」。而本章開頭所説的「曲」，「枉」，「窪」，「敝」，也都具有「不爭」的內涵。

TO SEEK LITTLE IS TO GAIN MUCH;

HE'S GOT THE DAO.

HE HAS THE VIRTUE.

TO SEEK MUCH IS TO BRING CONFUSION.

THEREFORE, THE SAGE PRESERVES THE DAO, BECOMING A MODEL FOR ALL THE WORLD.

BY NOT DISPLAYING HIMSELF, HE APPEARS BRIGHTEST. BY NOT INSISTING HE'S RIGHT, THE TRUTH IS MADE MANIFEST. BY NOT BOASTING OF ACHIEVEMENTS, ACHIEVEMENTS ARE NOTICED. BY NOT BEING PROUD, HE ENDURES.

IT IS BECAUSE HE DOESN'T CONTEND THAT NO ONE CAN CONTEND WITH HIM. THE ANCIENTS SAID, "TO BEND IS TO STAY WHOLE." WERE THESE JUST EMPTY WORDS?

PEOPLE ALWAYS PURSUE THE OUTWARD APPEARANCE OF THINGS, PURSUE WHOLENESS AND FULLNESS, AND BECAUSE OF THIS, THEY INVITE CONTENTION. WE SHOULD TRY TO RESIDE IN HUMILITY AND WEAKNESS, YIELDING AND RETREATING. IN THIS WAY, WE CAN ATTAIN A REALM OF NONCONTENTION.

● 佳：「美好」，「美利」，「銳利」的意思。「佳兵」是指銳利的兵器。

● 物或惡之：人所怨惡。「物」，即人。

● 「君子」居則貴左，用兵則貴右：古時候的人認為左陽右陰，陽生而陰殺。後文所謂「貴左」，「貴右」，「尚左」、「尚右」、「居左」、「居右」都是古時候的禮儀。

● 恬淡：安靜。

「武力是帶來凶災的東西。」老子指出了戰爭的禍害，而表達了他的反戰思想。

用兵是出於「不得已」的——若是為了除暴救民而用兵，也應該「恬淡為上」「戰勝了不要得意洋洋，得意洋洋就是喜歡殺人。」這話對於尚武者的心理狀態與行為樣態，真是一語道破。他還說：如果不得已而應戰，要「以喪禮處之，殺人之眾，以悲哀泣之。」這是人道主義的呼聲。

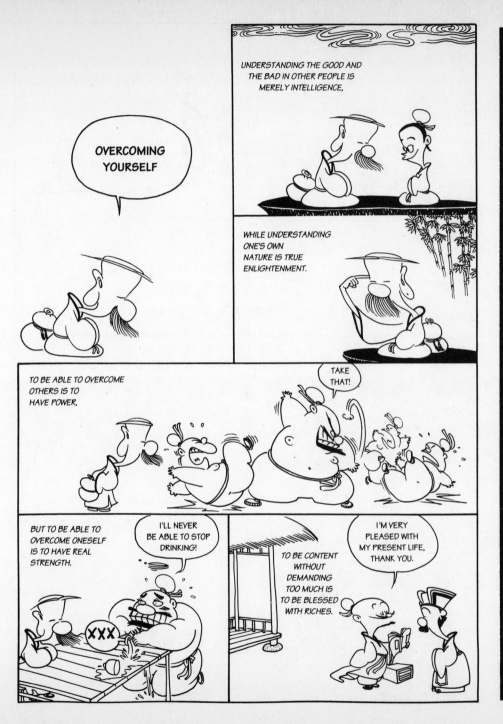

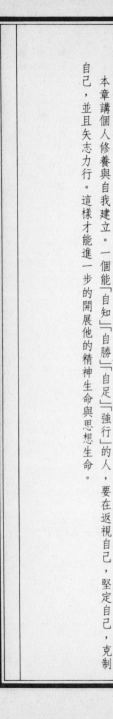

道

ONE WHO CAN UNDERSTAND THE DAO AND PERSEVERES IN ITS APPLICATION IS A PERSON OF STRONG WILL.

THE DAO!

道 DAO

ONE WHO CAN TAKE THE DAO AS A BASIS AND PRESERVE IT IS ONE WHO WILL ENDURE.

AND WHEN HE DIES, HIS SPIRIT WILL LIVE FOREVER. THIS IS TRUE LONGEVITY.

DAO

DAO

DAO

DAO

DAO

DAO

DAO

DAO

DAO

DAO

DAO

EVERYONE IS SELFISH AND HAS DESIRES. IF WE WISH TO RID OURSELVES OF SELFISH DESIRES, WE MUST FIRST ENGAGE IN SELF-EXAMINATION, AND THEN WE MUST PURIFY AND EMPTY OURSELVES. IF WE CAN UNDERSTAND OURSELVES, OVERCOME OURSELVES, BE CONTENT, AND PERSEVERE, THEN WE WILL HAVE ATTAINED THE DAO.

本章講個人修養與自我建立。一個能「自知」「自勝」「自足」「強行」的人，要在返視自己，堅定自己，克制自己，並且矢志力行。這樣才能進一步的開展他的精神生命與思想生命。

64

HOLDING ON TO THE DAO

IF YOU CAN HOLD ON TO THE DAO, THE WORLD WILL COME TO YOU.

IF THERE IS INTERACTION WITHOUT INCIDENT, THEN THERE WILL BE PEACE AMONG ALL.

GOOD MUSIC AND GOOD FOOD CAN HALT A PASSERBY.

THE DAO IS FLAVORLESS AND SILENT. ALTHOUGH YOU CANNOT SEE IT OR HEAR IT, IT IS INEXHAUSTIBLE IN ITS USEFULNESS.

GOVERNMENT BY BENEVOLENCE, RIGHTEOUSNESS, PROPRIETY, AND LAW IS LIKE GOOD MUSIC AND GOOD FOOD, WHICH ONLY FULFILL PEOPLE'S PHYSICAL DESIRES. THE DAO FULFILLS OUR SPIRITUAL NEEDS.

◉ 大象：大道。

◉ 安平太：「安」，乃：「太」，同泰，安、寧的意思。

◉ 樂與餌：音樂和美食。

◉ 既：盡。

65

THE STRENGTH OF WEAKNESS

TO SHRINK SOMETHING, FIRST EXPAND IT.
TO WEAKEN SOMETHING, FIRST STRENGTHEN IT.
TO ELIMINATE SOMETHING, FIRST GLORIFY IT.
TO OBTAIN SOMETHING, FIRST GIVE SOMETHING.

THIS IS ALL SO CLEAR. WEAKNESS WILL ALWAYS OVERCOME STRENGTH.

IF A FISH LEAVES THE DEPTHS, IT WILL DIE.

WEAKNESS IS THE FOUNDATION OF GOVERNMENT, AND IF IT IS NOT USED, THE NATION WILL BE LOST.

COERCION AND PUNISHMENT ARE EVIL MEANS THAT MUST NOT BE USED UPON THE PEOPLE.

"EVERYTHING REVERSES DIRECTION UPON REACHING ITS EXTREME" AND "THE STRONG SHALL BE WEAKENED" ARE ANCIENT SAYINGS. IF YOU UNDERSTAND AND EMPLOY THE PRINCIPLE BEHIND THEM, YOU TOO WILL BE ABLE TO OVERCOME STRENGTH WITH WEAKNESS.

◉歙：歙，合。韓非喻老引作「翕」。「翕」和「歙」古字通用。

◉之：作「者」。

◉微明：幾先的徵兆。

◉利器：有幾種說法；一說利器指賞罰；一說利器指權道；一說利器指聖智仁義巧利。

◉示：炫耀。

66

BOOK II

THE VIRTUE

● 上德不德：上『德』的人，因任自然，不表現為形式上的『德』。

● 下德不失德：下『德』的人，執守着形式上的『德』。

● 上德無為而無以為：上『德』的人，順任自然而無心作為。

● 下德無為而有以為：下『德』的人，順任自然而有心作為。

● 攘臂而扔之：伸出手臂來使人們強就。

●薄：衰薄，不足。
●亂之首：禍亂的開端。
●前識者：有先見的人；先知。
●華：虛華。

●處其厚：立身敦厚。河上公註：「「處其厚」者，處身於敦樸。」
●薄：澆薄，指「禮」。
●去彼取此：捨棄薄華的「禮」，採取厚實的「道」與「德」。

◉『有』：和一章「有」名萬物之母」的『有』相同。但和二章「有無相生」及十一章「有之以為利」的「有」不同。二與十一章上的「有」，是指現象界的具體存在物；而本章的『有』是意指超現象界的形上之『道』。

◉『無』：和一章「無」名天地之始」的『無』相同。但和二章「有無相生」與十一章「無之以為用」的「無」不同。二章與十一章上的「無」，是指現象界的非具體存在物；本章的『無』是意指超越現象界的形上之『道』。

> GETTING SOMETHING FROM NOTHING

THE DAO MOVES IN CYCLES OVER AND OVER, FLOWING UNCEASINGLY, AND IN THIS WAY, GIVES RISE TO THE ENDLESS FLOURISHING OF LIFE.

THE FUNCTIONING OF THE DAO IS WEAK AND HUMBLE.

THE MYRIAD THINGS UNDER HEAVEN ARE GENERATED FROM BEING.

BEING

AND BEING ARISES FROM NOTHING.

NOTHING

> NOTHING IS THE SUBSTANCE OF THE DAO, AND BEING IS ITS FUNCTION. IN ORDER TO ACHIEVE THE REALM OF THE DAO, WE MUST FIRST RECONCILE OURSELVES WITH NON-ACTION, NOT ENGAGING IN AFFAIRS OF THE WORLD, NON-INTELLECTUALIZING, NO-KNOWLEDGE, NO-DESIRES, EGOLESSNESS, AND SELFLESSNESS.

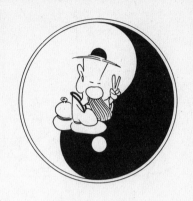

UNIVERSAL HARMONY

THE DAO IS THE UNDERLYING PRINCIPLE BEHIND THE CREATION OF THE MYRIAD THINGS. THE ORDER OF THE PROCESS THAT GIVES RISE TO THE MYRIAD THINGS BEGAN WITH THE DAO PRODUCING A KIND OF GENERATIVE FORCE.

DAO

THIS FORCE GAVE RISE TO THE TWO FORCES OF THE YIN AND YANG.

THE INTERACTION OF THE YIN AND YANG LED TO A STATE OF DYNAMIC BALANCE...

FROM WHICH THE MYRIAD THINGS ISSUED FORTH.

THE MYRIAD THINGS HAVE THEIR BACKS TO THE YIN AND FACE THE YANG. THROUGH THE BLENDING OF THE YIN AND YANG, A NEW HARMONY IS CREATED.

THE DAO CREATED THE MYRIAD THINGS, AND AFTER THEIR CREATION, THEY MUST STILL PRESERVE THE SPIRIT OF THE DAO AND ACT IN HARMONY WITH THE DAO. WE, TOO, SHOULD BE YIELDING AND ACT IN ACCORDANCE WITH NATURE.

●一：『道』是絕對無偶的，用數來表示為『一』。
●二：指陰氣、陽氣。
●三：有兩種說法：㈠陰陽相合所形成的一個均調和諧的狀態。㈡陰陽相合而形成「和氣」。

●負陰而抱陽：背陰而向陽。
●沖氣以為和：陰陽兩氣互相交沖而形成均調和諧狀態。

72

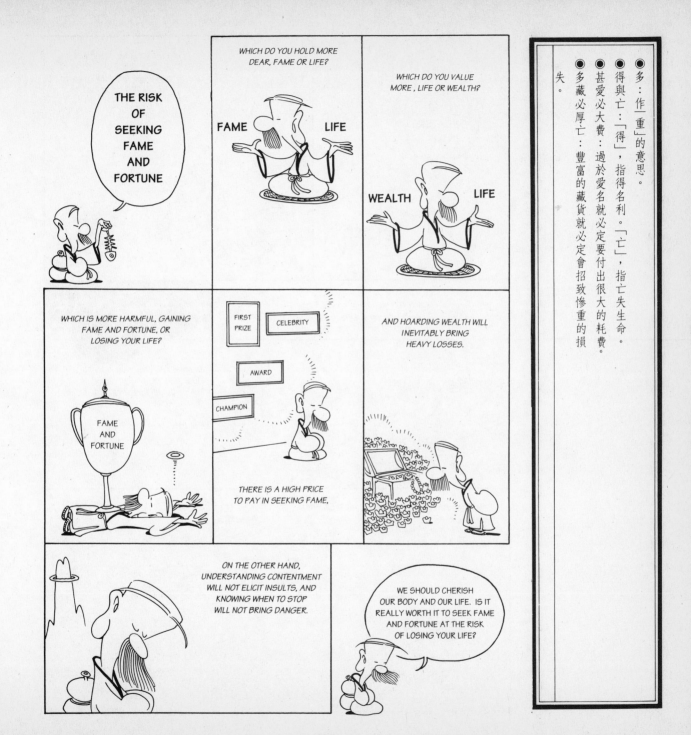

OUR COUNTRY IS SO SMALL, AND THE NEIGHBORING COUNTRIES ARE SO BIG...

WE'RE BIG ENOUGH! THERE'S NO NEED TO BE GREEDY...

NO, WE'RE TOO SMALL!

ATTACK! GET SOME OF THEIR LAND!

THERE IS NO GREATER DISASTER THAN DISCONTENTMENT. THERE IS NO GREATER CRIME THAN GREED.

THE ONLY LASTING SATISFACTION IS THAT WHICH IS FOUND IN KNOWING WHEN ENOUGH IS ENOUGH. IF EVERYONE WERE CONTENTED, THE WORLD WOULD BE A PEACEFUL PLACE.

戰爭的起因，大半由於侵略者的野心勃勃，貪得而不知止足，結果侵入國土，傷人性命，帶來無窮的災難。老子指陳統治者多欲生事的為害，警惕為政者當清靜無為，收斂侵佔的意欲。「天下無道，戎馬生於郊。」也可反映出當時兵馬倥傯，互相殺伐的慘烈情況。本章和三十章、三十一章都含有反戰思想，沉痛抨擊當時的武力侵略。

75

● 天道：自然的規律。

● 不見而明：「明」原作「名」，「名」與「明」古時通用。

● 不為：即無為，不妄為。

●為學日益：為學是指探求外物的知識活動。這裡的「為學」，範圍較狹，僅指對於仁義聖智禮法的追求。這些學問是能增加人的知見與智巧的。

●為道日損：「為道」是通過暝想或體驗以領悟事物未分化狀態的『道』。這裡的『道』是指自然之『道』，無為之『道』。

●無為而無不為：不妄為，就沒有什麼事情做不成的。

●無事：即是無擾攘之事。

●有事：繁苛政舉。這裡的「事」，猶如「惹事生非」的「事」。

常心：成見。

●德：假借為「得」。

●歙歙焉：「歙」，收歙，指收歙意欲。

●渾其心：使人心思化歸於渾樸。

●聖人皆孩之：「聖人」使他們都回復到嬰孩般真純的狀態。

●百姓皆注其耳目：百姓都專注他們自己的耳目。指百姓競相用智，自然會產生各種的紛爭。

THE SAGE HOLDS NO PREJUDICE. HE TAKES THE PEOPLE'S OPINIONS AS HIS OWN.

THE IDEAL LEADER

I AM GOOD TO GOOD PEOPLE AND BAD PEOPLE ALIKE. IN THIS WAY, I CAN CAUSE THE PEOPLE TO BE GOOD.

GOOD!

I TRUST TRUSTWORTHY PEOPLE, AND I TRUST UNTRUSTWORTHY PEOPLE. IN THIS WAY, I CAN CAUSE THE PEOPLE TO BE TRUSTWORTHY.

TRUSTWORTHY!

WHEN A SAGE IS GOVERNING, HE RESTRAINS HIS DESIRES, MAKING THE PEOPLE SIMPLE AND INNOCENT. THE PEOPLE STARE AND LISTEN QUIETLY, AS THOUGH IGNORANT OR DUMB. THE SAGE PROTECTS THEM AS HE WOULD INFANTS.

THE IDEAL RULER RESTRAINS HIS DESIRES, DOESN'T CODIFY HIS OWN SUBJECTIVE STANDARDS OF RIGHT AND WRONG, AND TREATS ALL PEOPLE WITH GOODNESS AND SINCERITY.

● 出生入死：人出世為「生」，入地為「死」。
● 生之徒：屬於長命的。「徒」，類，屬。
● 十有三：十分中有三分：即十分之三。
● 死之徒：屬於夭折的。

● 人之生，動之於死地：人本來可以得生，但是卻走向了死路。
● 生生之厚：求生太過度了，酒肉饜飽，奢侈淫佚，奉養過厚了。

79

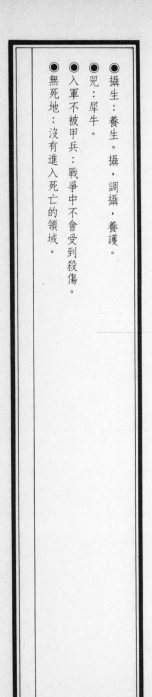

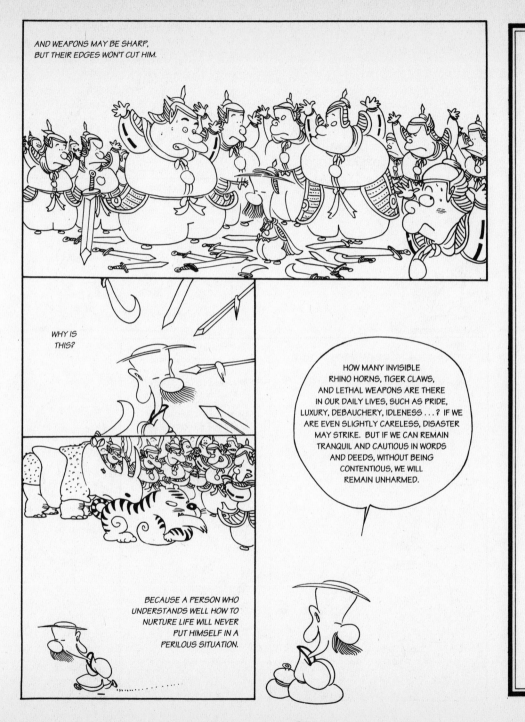

AND WEAPONS MAY BE SHARP, BUT THEIR EDGES WON'T CUT HIM.

WHY IS THIS?

HOW MANY INVISIBLE RHINO HORNS, TIGER CLAWS, AND LETHAL WEAPONS ARE THERE IN OUR DAILY LIVES, SUCH AS PRIDE, LUXURY, DEBAUCHERY, IDLENESS...? IF WE ARE EVEN SLIGHTLY CARELESS, DISASTER MAY STRIKE. BUT IF WE CAN REMAIN TRANQUIL AND CAUTIOUS IN WORDS AND DEEDS, WITHOUT BEING CONTENTIOUS, WE WILL REMAIN UNHARMED.

BECAUSE A PERSON WHO UNDERSTANDS WELL HOW TO NURTURE LIFE WILL NEVER PUT HIMSELF IN A PERILOUS SITUATION.

人生在世，大約有十分之三是長壽的，十分之三是短命的，這些都是屬於自然的死亡。另有十分之三的人，本來可以活得長久，但是貪饜好得，傷殘身體，而自己糟塌了生命。只有極少數（十分之一）的人，善於護養自己的性命，能做到少私寡欲，過着清靜樸質、純任自然的生活。

●知者不言，言者不知：按字面的解釋是：知道的人不說話，說話的人不知道。深一層的意思是：智者是不〔向人民〕施加政令的，施加政令的人就不是智者。

●挫其銳，解其紛，和其光，同其塵：不露鋒芒，消解紛擾，含斂光耀，混同塵世。

●玄同：玄妙齊同的境界。即「道」的境界。

●不可得而親，不可得而疏，不可得而利，不可得

A WISE PERSON UNDERSTANDS THE SUBTLETY AND MYSTERY OF THE DAO AND SO CAUTIOUSLY PUTS IT INTO PRACTICE, NOT DARING TO BE TOO TALKATIVE.

THOSE WHO PRATTLE ON AND ON UNDERSTAND NOTHING ABOUT THE DAO.

ONE WHO SPEAKS DOES NOT KNOW

DO NOT REVEAL YOUR SHARPNESS; ELIMINATE ALL COMPLICATIONS; WITHHOLD YOUR BRIGHTNESS; MERGE WITH THE DUSTY WORLD. THIS IS THE REALM OF MYSTERIOUS IDENTITY.

BY TRANSCENDING THE MATERIAL WORLD AND BEING TRANQUIL, NO ONE CAN GET TOO CLOSE TO YOU, NO ONE CAN ALIENATE YOU, NO ONE CAN BENEFIT YOU, NO ONE CAN HARM YOU, NO ONE CAN HONOR YOU, AND NO ONE CAN DEBASE YOU. THIS IS THE HIGHEST REALM THAT CAN BE ATTAINED BY ANY PERSON.

BY BEING HUMBLE AND UNTROUBLED, WE CONTROL OUR OWN CIRCUMSTANCES, AND NO ONE ELSE CAN MAKE OR BREAK US.

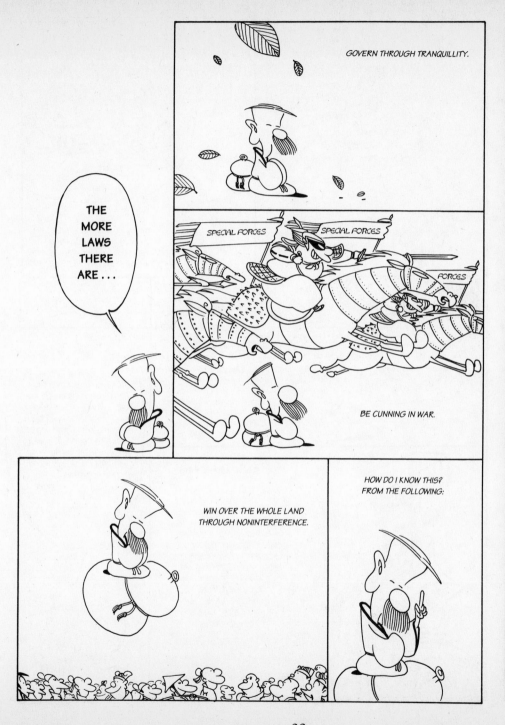

GOVERN THROUGH TRANQUILLITY.

THE MORE LAWS THERE ARE...

SPECIAL FORCES

SPECIAL FORCES

FORCES

BE CUNNING IN WAR.

WIN OVER THE WHOLE LAND THROUGH NONINTERFERENCE.

HOW DO I KNOW THIS? FROM THE FOLLOWING:

而害，不可得而貴，不可得而賤：：指『玄同』的境界超出了親疏利害貴賤的區別。

● 正：指清靜之道。
● 奇：奇巧，詭秘。臨機應變。
● 取天下：治理天下。
● 以此：以這些事情。「此」指下面一段文字。

● 忌諱：防禁。
● 利器：指權謀。
● 伎巧：技巧，即智巧
● 奇物：邪事。
● 自化：自我化育。

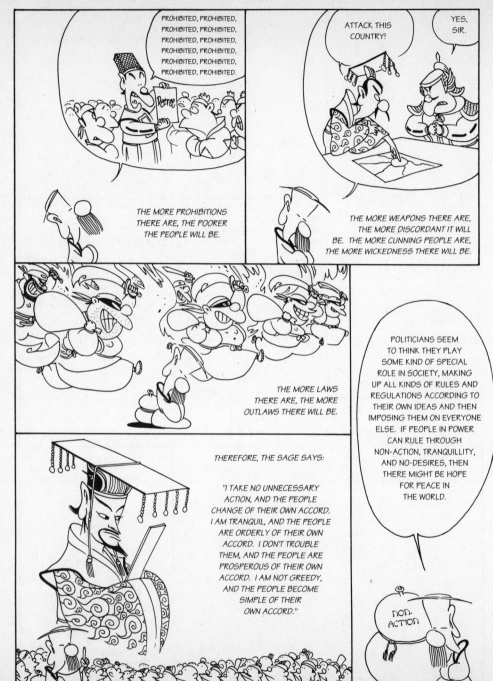

PROHIBITED, PROHIBITED, PROHIBITED, PROHIBITED, PROHIBITED, PROHIBITED, PROHIBITED, PROHIBITED, PROHIBITED, PROHIBITED, PROHIBITED, PROHIBITED, PROHIBITED, PROHIBITED.

THE MORE PROHIBITIONS THERE ARE, THE POORER THE PEOPLE WILL BE.

ATTACK THIS COUNTRY!

YES, SIR.

THE MORE WEAPONS THERE ARE, THE MORE DISCORDANT IT WILL BE. THE MORE CUNNING PEOPLE ARE, THE MORE WICKEDNESS THERE WILL BE.

THE MORE LAWS THERE ARE, THE MORE OUTLAWS THERE WILL BE.

THEREFORE, THE SAGE SAYS:

"I TAKE NO UNNECESSARY ACTION, AND THE PEOPLE CHANGE OF THEIR OWN ACCORD. I AM TRANQUIL, AND THE PEOPLE ARE ORDERLY OF THEIR OWN ACCORD. I DON'T TROUBLE THEM, AND THE PEOPLE ARE PROSPEROUS OF THEIR OWN ACCORD. I AM NOT GREEDY, AND THE PEOPLE BECOME SIMPLE OF THEIR OWN ACCORD."

POLITICIANS SEEM TO THINK THEY PLAY SOME KIND OF SPECIAL ROLE IN SOCIETY, MAKING UP ALL KINDS OF RULES AND REGULATIONS ACCORDING TO THEIR OWN IDEAS AND THEN IMPOSING THEM ON EVERYONE ELSE. IF PEOPLE IN POWER CAN RULE THROUGH NON-ACTION, TRANQUILLITY, AND NO-DESIRES, THEN THERE MIGHT BE HOPE FOR PEACE IN THE WORLD.

NON-ACTION

FRYING FISH

GOVERNING A LARGE COUNTRY IS LIKE FRYING A SMALL FISH—YOU CAN'T TURN IT OVER TOO OFTEN.

IF TURNED OVER TOO MANY TIMES, THE FISH WILL FALL APART.

BY GOVERNING THROUGH TRANQUILLITY AND NON-ACTION, THE GODS AND SPIRITS REMAIN IN THEIR PROPER PLACES. SO THE SPIRITS DO NOT HARM PEOPLE,

AND NEITHER DO THE GODS.

SAGES ALSO DO NOT HARM THE PEOPLE.

IF THE RULER AND THE PEOPLE DO NOT HARM EACH OTHER, THERE WILL BE PEACE THROUGHOUT THE LAND.

IF A RULER CAN LEAD THROUGH TRANQUILLITY AND NOT INTERFERE WITH THE LIVES OF THE PEOPLE, AND IF THE RULER CAN MAINTAIN SERENITY AND NON-ACTION, THEN THE PEOPLE CAN GO ABOUT THEIR OWN LIVES AND BE PEACEFUL AND PROSPEROUS OF THEMSELVES.

◉ 其神不傷人：伸於陽者不傷民。

◉ 兩不相傷：指鬼神和聖人不侵越人。

◉ 小鮮：小魚。

◉ 莅：同「涖」，臨。

◉ 其鬼不神：鬼不起作用。古人常用陰陽和順來說明國泰民安，古人以陰氣過盛稱「鬼」。「神」這裡作「伸」講。

◉ 德交歸焉：意即人民相安無事。

◉百谷王：百川所歸往。「百谷」，即百川。

◉重：累，不堪。

NAVIGATING
THE STATE

THE OCEAN IS THE KING OF ALL RIVERS AND CAUSES THEM ALL TO COME RUNNING INTO ITSELF BECAUSE IT SKILLFULLY STAYS BELOW THEM.

SO IN LEADING THE PEOPLE, A SAGE MUST ALSO PUT HIMSELF BELOW. TO BE AHEAD OF THE PEOPLE, HE MUST PUT HIMSELF BEHIND THEM.

THEREFORE, WHILE THE SAGE RESIDES ABOVE THE PEOPLE, THE PEOPLE DO NOT FEEL BURDENED, AND WITH HIM AT THE FRONT, THE PEOPLE DO NOT FEEL THREATENED. IN THIS WAY, THE PEOPLE WILL GLADLY SUPPORT AND RESPECT THEIR LEADER AND NOT LOATHE AND FORSAKE HIM.

BECAUSE HE DOES NOT CONTEND, NO ONE CAN CONTEND WITH HIM.

IF A LEADER TAKES ADVANTAGE OF HIS POWER, HE IS TAKING ADVANTAGE OF THE PEOPLE. A GOOD LEADER REMEMBERS THAT HE IS A SERVANT OF THE PEOPLE.

● 士：這裡作將帥講。
● 不與：不爭。
● 配天古之極：最合自然的道理

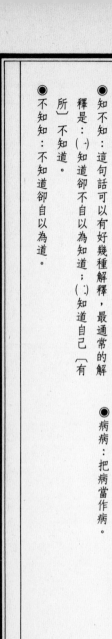

◉勇於敢則殺，勇於不敢則活：勇於堅強就會死，勇於柔弱就可活。
◉此兩者或利或害：指勇於柔弱則利，勇於堅強則有害。

◉天之道：自然的規律。
◉繟然：坦然，安然，寬緩。
◉天網：自然的範圍。
◉恢恢：寬大，廣大。
◉失：漏失。

◉柔弱：指人體的柔軟。

◉堅強：指人體的僵硬。

◉柔脆：指草木形質的柔軟脆弱。

◉枯槁：形容草木的乾枯。

◉死之徒：屬於死亡的一類。

◉生之徒：屬於生存的一類。

◉強梁者不得其死：強暴的人會不得好死。

TREE
VS.
GRASS

WHEN PEOPLE ARE ALIVE, THEIR BODIES ARE TENDER AND SOFT. WHEN DEAD, THEY BECOME STIFF AND HARD.

PLANTS ARE ALSO TENDER AND SUPPLE WHEN ALIVE.

ONLY TO BECOME DRY AND BRITTLE WHEN THEY DIE.

STIFF AND HARD THINGS BELONG TO THE REALM OF THE DEAD,

WHILE THE TENDER AND SOFT BELONG TO THE REALM OF THE LIVING.

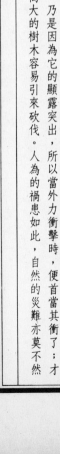

老子從人類和草木的生存現象中，說明成長的東西都是柔弱的狀態，而死亡的東西都是堅硬的狀態。老子從萬物活動所觀察到的物理之恆情，而斷言：「堅強者死之徒，柔弱者生之徒。」老子的結論還蘊涵着堅強的東西已失去了生機，柔弱的東西則充滿着生機。這是從事物的內在發展狀況來說明的。若從它們外在表現上來說，堅強者之所以屬於死之徒，乃是因為它的顯露突出，所以當外力衝擊時，才能外露，容易招忌而遭致掊擊，這正如高大的樹木容易引來砍伐。人為的禍患如此，自然的災難亦莫不然

NOTHING IS MORE PLIANT THAN WATER.

WATER VS. ROCK

AND NOTHING CAN ATTACK HARD AND STRONG THINGS BETTER.

SO THE SAGE SAYS, "ONLY THE PERSON WHO CAN SHOULDER THE DISGRACES AND DISASTERS OF A COUNTRY IS FIT TO BE ITS LEADER."

THE WEAK OVERCOMES THE STRONG, THE SOFT OVERCOMES THE HARD. EVERYONE KNOWS THIS, BUT NO ONE IS ABLE TO PUT IT INTO PRACTICE.

THE NATURE OF WATER IS PLIANCY, AND YET THERE IS NO FIRMNESS IT CAN'T PENETRATE AND NO STRENGTH IT CAN'T OVERCOME. MAYBE WE CAN LEARN SOMETHING FROM WATER.

◉無以易之：沒有什麼能代替它。

◉受國之垢：承擔全國的屈辱。

◉受國不祥：承擔全國的禍難。

◉正言若反：正確的話聽來卻像反面的話。

●左契:「契」即券契,就像現在所謂的「合同」。古時候,刻木為契,剖分左右,各人存執一半,以求日後相合符信。左契是負債人訂立的,交給債權人收執,就像今天所說的借據存根。

●責:索取償還,即債權人以收執的左卷向負債人索取所欠的東西。

●司徹:掌管稅收。「徹」是周代的稅法。

●無親:沒有偏愛。

THE MORE YOU GIVE, THE MORE YOU GET

TRUE WORDS ARE NOT PLEASANT TO HEAR;

WORDS THAT ARE PLEASANT TO HEAR ARE NOT TRUE.

A GOOD PERSON DOES NOT ARGUE;

AN ARGUMENTATIVE PERSON IS NOT GOOD.

A WISE PERSON UNDERSTANDS THAT THE GREAT DAO OF THE UNIVERSE LIES WITHIN ONE'S OWN HEART AND THAT IT ISN'T NECESSARY TO RUN AROUND IN SEARCH OF IT.

● 信言：真話，由衷之言。
● 美言：動聽的話。
● 善者：可以解釋為行為良善的人，也可以解釋為善於言說的人。

A PERSON OF BROAD KNOWLEDGE DOESN'T NECESSARILY UNDERSTAND THE GREAT DAO.

THE MORE HE GIVES TO OTHERS, THE MORE HE HAS.

THE HEAVENLY DAO IS NOT SELFISH. IT ONLY BENEFITS THE MYRIAD THINGS AND DOES NOT HARM THEM.

THE SAGE IS UNSELFISH, KEEPING NOTHING FOR HIMSELF. THE MORE HE HELPS OTHERS, THE MORE HE GAINS.

THE SAGE ACTS IN ACCORDANCE WITH THE DAO, PROVIDING WITHOUT CONTENDING.

THE SAGE "HELPS WITHOUT HARMING" AND "ACTS WITHOUT CONTENDING." AS A RESULT, "NOTHING AND NO ONE CAN CONTEND WITH HIM." THE SAYING "TO GIVE IS BETTER THAN TO RECEIVE" DEMONSTRATES THIS NONCONTENTIOUS SPIRIT AND EXHIBITS, AS WELL, THE SPIRIT OF THE DAO.

ANCIENT THINKERS DISCUSS THE DAO

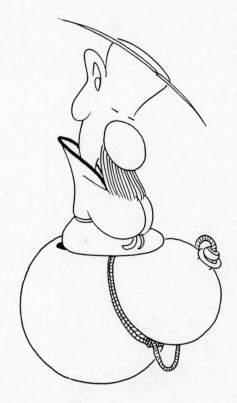

『道』這個字，在老子書上前後出現了七十三次，這七十三個『道』字，符號型式雖然一樣，但是意義內容却不盡同。

100

"PEOPLE FOLLOW THE EARTH, THE EARTH FOLLOWS HEAVEN, HEAVEN FOLLOWS THE DAO, THE DAO FOLLOWS NATURE."

—DAO DE JING, CHAP. 25

有物混成，先天地生。……吾不知其名，強字之曰「道」，強為之名曰大。……

故「道」大，天大，地大，人亦大。域中有四大，而人居其一焉。

人法地，地法天，天法「道」，「道」法自然。

本章所說的「道」，都是指實存意義的道。末句所說的「天法『道』，『道』法自然」，乃是指效法實存之『道』所呈現的自然規律。

本章談『道』，老子認為不妄為，也不故意表現他的作為（「無為而無以為」），可以稱為「上德」。如果妄自作為，而且故意表現他的作為（「為之而有以為」），那就變成「下德」了。「上德」者，因任自然，體『道』而行。如果表現「有為」（妄自作為），那就失『道』了。失『道』是有為的結果。「失道」的『道』，即是指自然無為的『道』。「道之華」的『道』，也是承接上文指自然無為的『道』。

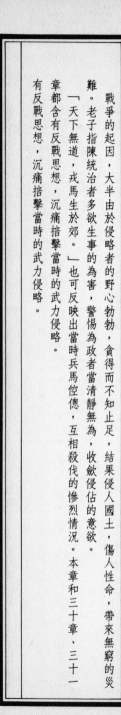

"THERE IS NO GREATER DISASTER THAN DISCONTENTMENT. THERE IS NO GREATER CRIME THAN GREED."

—DAO DE JING, CHAP. 46

「知」作「智」解。嚴靈峯先生說：「此兩「智」字，原俱作「知」；似當讀去聲，作「智慧」之「智」。陸德明釋文云：「「知」者，或並音「智」。」……河上公注「智者不言」句云：「知者貴行不貴言也。」王註云：「因自然也。」又何上注『言者不知』句云：「馳不及舌，多言多患。」王註云：「造事端也。」疑河上，王弼兩本「知」皆作『智』者。

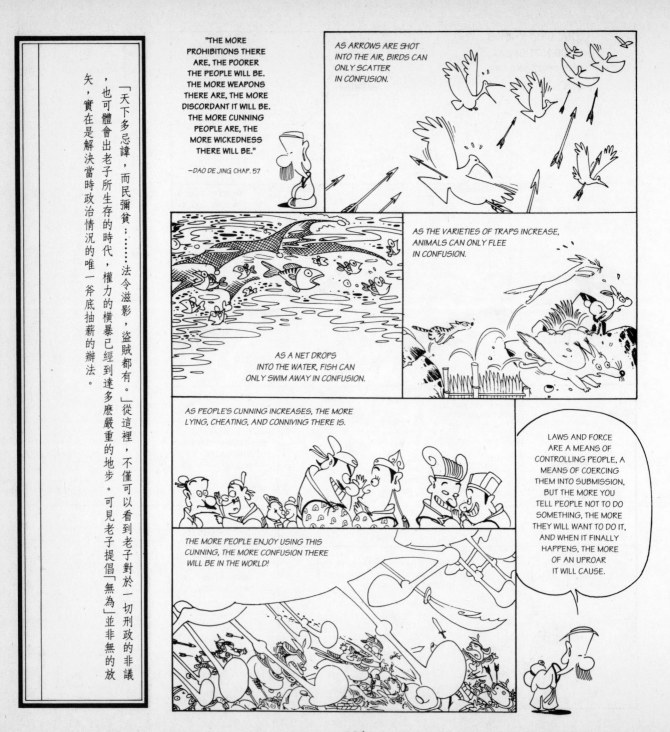

"THE MORE PROHIBITIONS THERE ARE, THE POORER THE PEOPLE WILL BE. THE MORE WEAPONS THERE ARE, THE MORE DISCORDANT IT WILL BE. THE MORE CUNNING PEOPLE ARE, THE MORE WICKEDNESS THERE WILL BE."

–DAO DE JING CHAP. 57

AS ARROWS ARE SHOT INTO THE AIR, BIRDS CAN ONLY SCATTER IN CONFUSION.

AS THE VARIETIES OF TRAPS INCREASE, ANIMALS CAN ONLY FLEE IN CONFUSION.

AS A NET DROPS INTO THE WATER, FISH CAN ONLY SWIM AWAY IN CONFUSION.

AS PEOPLE'S CUNNING INCREASES, THE MORE LYING, CHEATING, AND CONNIVING THERE IS.

THE MORE PEOPLE ENJOY USING THIS CUNNING, THE MORE CONFUSION THERE WILL BE IN THE WORLD!

LAWS AND FORCE ARE A MEANS OF CONTROLLING PEOPLE, A MEANS OF COERCING THEM INTO SUBMISSION, BUT THE MORE YOU TELL PEOPLE NOT TO DO SOMETHING, THE MORE THEY WILL WANT TO DO IT, AND WHEN IT FINALLY HAPPENS, THE MORE OF AN UPROAR IT WILL CAUSE.

「天下多忌諱，而民彌貧；……法令滋彰，盜賊都有。」從這裡，不僅可以看到老子對於一切刑政的非議，也可體會出老子所生存的時代，權力的橫暴已經到達多麼嚴重的地步。可見老子提倡「無為」並非無的放矢，實在是解決當時政治情況的唯一斧底抽薪的辦法。

Corresponding Chapters in the *Dao De Jing*

Page 28 of this book corresponds to chapter 1 of the *Dao De Jing* . . .

32	2
34	3
36	4
37	5
39	7
40	8
42	9
44	10
45	11
47	12
49	13
51	16
53	17
55	18
56	20
59	22
61	31
63	33
65	35
66	36
68	38
70	40
71	42
72	43
73	44
74	46
76	47
77	48
78	49
79	50
82	56
83	57
85	60
86	66
87	68
88	71
89	73
91	76
93	78
94	79
95	81

Guide to Pronunciation

There are different systems of Romanization of Chinese words, but in all of these systems the sounds of letters used do not necessarily correspond to those sounds which we are accustomed to in English (for instance, would you have guessed that *zh* is pronounced like *jth* ?). Of course these systems can be learned, but to save some time and effort for the reader who is not a student of Chinese, we have provided the following pronunciation guide. The Chinese words appear on the left as they do in the text and are followed by their pronunciations. Just sound out the pronunciations intuitively and you will be quite close to the proper Mandarin Chinese pronunciations.

Notes:
-dz is a combination of *d* and *z* in one sound, without the *ee* sound at the end; so it sounds kind of like a bee in flight with a slight *d* sound at the beginning.
-ts is mostly the *ss* sound with a slight *t* (minus the *ee*) sound at the beginning.

Bo Ju: bwo (*o* as in m*o*re)-jew (*ew* as in f*ew*)
Bohun Wuren: bwo (*o* as in m*o*re)-hwoon (*oo* as in b*oo*k) oo-run

Chu: choo

Dan: don
Dao: dow
Dou: dough

Er: are
fa jia: fa (as in *fa*ther)-jyah

Han: hon (rhymes with gone)
Hu: hoo
Huang Di: hwong dee
Huang-Lao: hwong-lou (*lou* as in *lou*nge)
Huineng: hway-nung

Ji Shengzi: jee shung-dz

Kongzi: kong (long *o*)-dz

Laozi: lou (as in *lou*nge)-dz
Li: lee
Liang: lyong
Liezi: lyeh-dz
Luoyang: lwo (*o* as in m*o*re)-yong

Mawangdui: ma-wong-dway

Qi: chee
Qin: cheen
Quren: chew (rhymes with f*ew*)-run

rou dao: roe dow

Shi: sure
Shi Chengqi: sure chung-chee

Tai Shang Lao Jun: tie shong lou (as in *lou*nge) jewn (*ew* as in f*ew*)

Tsai Chih Chung: tsigh (rhymes with high) jir jong (long *o*)
Wu: oo
Wu Wei: oo way
Wujincang: oo-jeen-tsong

Yang Zhu: yong joo
Yin Yang: een yong
Yin Xi: een shee

Zhao: jow (as in *jow*l)
Zhou: joe
Zhuangzi: jwong-dz